AUGUST STRINDBERG

Miss Julie

translated by
MICHAEL MEYER

with commentary and notes by
DAVID THOMAS *and* JO TAYLOR

METHUEN DRAMA

Methuen Drama Student Edition

10 9 8 7 6 5

This edition first published in the United Kingdom in 2006 by
Methuen Publishing Ltd

Reissued with a new cover design 2009

Methuen Drama
A & C Black Publishers Limited
36 Soho Square
London W1D 3QY
www.methuendrama.com

This translation of *Miss Julie* first published in 1964 by Secker & Warburg Ltd and
subsequently in 1976 by Eyre Methuen Ltd in a revised edition

Copyright © 1964, 1987 by the Estate of Michael Meyer

Commentary and notes copyright © 2006 by David Thomas and Jo Taylor

Under the provisions of the Copyright, Designs and Patents Act, 1988, Michael
Meyer, David Thomas and Jo Taylor have asserted their rights to be identified
respectively as the translator of the play and authors of the Commentary and Notes

A CIP catalogue record for this book is available from the British Library

ISBN 978 0 413 77582 5

Available in the USA from Bloomsbury Academic & Professional,
175 Fifth Avenue/3rd Floor, New York, NY 10010.
www.BloomsburyAcademicUSA.com

Typeset by SX Composing DTP, Rayleigh, Essex
Printed and bound in Great Britain by CPI Cox & Wyman, Reading, Berkshire

Contents

Johan August Strindberg: 1849–1912

1849 Johan August Strindberg born in Stockholm on 22 January, fourth son of Carl Oscar Strindberg (a shipping agent) and his wife Ulrika Eleonora (née Norling) who was previously his serving woman.

1853 August's father goes bankrupt, although later recovered some financial stability. His financial embarrassment aggravated his already irascible temper.

1862 August's mother dies. Thereafter she becomes for him a symbol of ideal purity.

1863 August's father marries his young housekeeper, Emilia Peterson. August is mortified by this, which he sees as an act of betrayal.

1867 After passing the Student Matriculation Examination, Strindberg spends the summer term at Uppsala University where he decides to study Medicine.

1868 Returns to Stockholm and supports himself as a supply teacher and private tutor.

1869 Fails his preliminary examination in Medicine. Shortly afterwards engaged as a trainee actor at Stockholm's Royal Dramatic Theatre (Dramaten), but he also fails at that. He writes his earliest plays, of which two have survived, *The Freethinker* and *Hermione*.

1870 Returns to Uppsala University to study Humanities (Modern Languages and Political Science). His fourth play *In Rome* is performed briefly at Dramaten.

1871 His play *The Outlaw* is performed at Dramaten. He receives a small grant from King Karl XV who had enjoyed this latest play. The royal grant permits Strindberg to continue his studies for a further year.

1872 Leaves Uppsala without completing his degree course. Settles in Stockholm and makes a second, unsuccessful attempt to become an actor. Completes his first major play, the prose version of *Master Olof*, a historical drama

set in Sweden at the time of the Reformation. It was not
performed for nine years.

1872 Works as a journalist in Stockholm on various newspapers
-74 and briefly edits a journal for the insurance trade.

1874 Appointed as an assistant librarian at Stockholm's Royal
-82 Library and given the task of cataloguing the Library's
collection of Chinese manuscripts.

1875 After a brief emotional entanglement with Ina Forstén, the
fiancée of an old friend, becomes increasingly friendly with
Siri von Essen and her husband Baron Carl Gustaf Wrangel.

1876 Makes his first visit to Paris and writes a version of *Master
Olof* in verse. Becomes progressively more infatuated with
Siri von Essen.

1877 Marries Siri after her divorce from Baron Wrangel.

1878 Their first daughter dies shortly after birth.

1879 Publishes *The Red Room*, a novel satirising writers and
artists in contemporary Stockholm. This establishes his
literary reputation as a writer of substance, but it also
makes him many enemies.

1880 Birth of his daughter Karin.

1881 First performance of *Master Olof* at Dramaten in the
original prose version. Birth of his daughter Greta.

1882 After the success of *Master Olof*, Strindberg is inspired to
write, within a fortnight, a romantic fairy-tale play called
Lucky Peter's Journey. This too is a theatrical success.
Publishes *The New State*, a swingeing onslaught against
contemporary Swedish society and its politics. He is now
subjected to virulent attacks in the press.

1883 Leaves Sweden (in part because of these attacks) and lives
abroad in France, Switzerland, Germany and Denmark
until 1889.

1884 Publishes *Marriage I*, a collection of short stories about
married life. His critique of confirmation and communion
as devices to keep the lower classes in their place and his
irreverent comments on the wafers and wine distributed at
communion lead to him being prosecuted for blasphemy.
He returns to Stockholm for the trial. Although he is
acquitted, he is left feeling persecuted and diminished by
the experience. Birth of his son Hans.

1885 Publishes *Marriage II*, a deliberately anti-feminist collection of stories.

1886 Publishes the first two volumes of his autobiographical novel *The Son of a Serving Woman*. Also publishes his first attempt at a Naturalist play, *Comrades*.

1887 Writes *The Father* in southern Germany. It is performed in Denmark with some success but is not well received in Sweden. Writes a rustic novel called *The People of Hemsö*, about life in the Stockholm archipelago.

1888 Writes *Miss Julie* and *Comrades* while living in Denmark. In French, writes *A Madman's Defence*, a highly subjective account of his marriage to Siri. Corresponds with Nietzsche just before the latter becomes insane. *Miss Julie* is widely attacked for immorality when it is published and Strindberg is unable to find a theatre willing to perform it.

1889 Partly in response to this, founds his Scandinavian Experimental Theatre in Copenhagen, which is modelled on André Antoine's Théâtre Libre in Paris. *Miss Julie* is banned by the Danish censor the night before it opens and the production has to be transferred to the Copenhagen Students' Union. The production closes after two performances and the theatre goes bankrupt. Writes *The Stronger* and returns to Sweden.

1890 Writes *By the Open Sea*, a novel about the psychological collapse of an intellectual.

1891 Divorces Siri von Essen.

1892 Writes *Playing with Fire* and *The Bond*, his last plays for six years. After living in Stockholm or the archipelago with friends and family, leaves for Berlin. Joins the circle of bohemians and artists who gathered in a tavern called 'Zum schwarzen Ferkel' (The black piglet).

1893 Marries the young Austrian journalist Frida Uhl (she was twenty-one). They spend their honeymoon in England, then live in various places in Germany and with her relatives in Austria. *Miss Julie* staged by Antoine.

1894 After the birth of his daughter, Kerstin, separates from his second wife and moves to Paris. *Creditors* and *The Father* are staged in Paris. Strindberg is now seen there as a famous literary figure, but he remains impoverished.

1894   Writes articles on alchemy while attempting to make gold.
 –96   Suffers from paranoid hallucinations. Studies occultism,
       alchemy and theosophy. Begins to lose his grip on sanity.
       He called this period his Inferno crisis.
1895   Two stays as a voluntary patient at a psychiatric clinic in
 –96   Ystad, Sweden.
1896   Leaves Paris and returns to live in Lund, southern Sweden
       for the next three years.
1897   Writes *Inferno* in French, an autobiographical account of
       his breakdown. Divorces Frida Uhl.
1898   Writes *To Damascus*, Parts I and II. This gives a dramatic
       account, in Expressionist form, of his Inferno experience.
       Writes his mystery play *Advent*.
1899   Writes *There are Crimes and Crimes*, and *Erik XIV*, the first of
       many fine historical plays he is to write over the coming
       years. Moves to Stockholm.
1900   Writes *Gustav Adolf, Easter, The Bridal Crown*, and *Dance of
       Death* Parts I and II, a dark comedy that foreshadows
       Absurdist techniques. Meets the young Norwegian actress
       Harriet Bosse.
1901   Marries Harriet Bosse (she was twenty), but she leaves him
       before the end of the year. Devotes most of his *Occult Diary*
       (begun in 1897) to this failed relationship. Writes a fairy-
       tale play *Swanwhite*, followed by Part III of *To Damascus*
       and *A Dream Play*, an elegiac Expressionist piece exploring
       life's recurring patterns of absurdity and anguish. Also
       writes further historical plays, *Charles XII* and *Queen
       Christina*.
1902   Birth of his daughter Anne-Marie. Writes a historical play
       Gustav III.
1904   Divorces Harriet Bosse. Writes *Black Banners*, an outspoken
       attack on his fellow writers, thinly disguised as a novel.
1907   Writes various essays and articles on religion, philosophy
 –12   and politics, including cabalistic works, some of which
       were collected in his four *Blue Books*.
1907   With the young director August Falck, founds his own
       experimental theatre in Stockholm, Intima Teatern.
       Writes four atmospheric chamber plays for this theatre:
       Storm, The Burnt House, The Ghost Sonata, The Pelican. None

of them is understood by contemporary audiences, but *The Ghost Sonata* is now viewed as an Expressionist masterpiece. *Miss Julie* is given a triumphant, long-running production at Intima Teatern.

1908 Moves into a flat he called 'The Blue Tower' in Drottninggatan 85, Stockholm: this was to be his final home and is now the site of the Strindberg Museum.

1908 Writes *Open Letters to Intima Teatern*, a collection of
–09 essays on Shakespeare and other theatrical topics.

1909 Writes his last play *The Great Highway*, another Expressionist piece. Engaged briefly to Fanny Falkner, an art student (she was nineteen at the time).

1910 Intima Teatern closes.

1911 Signs a contract with the publisher Albert Bonniers for the publication of his collected works. For the first time in his life achieves financial security.

1912 In January, his sixty-third birthday is celebrated with a torchlight procession to his home and he is given a gift of 50,000 crowns. He is already suffering from terminal cancer. On 14 May he dies of cancer of the stomach. Workers and students accompany his funeral cortège to the New Church Cemetery where his grave, among the poor, is marked, in accordance with his last wishes, with a cross of dark oak bearing the inscription 'Ave Crux, Spes Unica' (Hail O Cross, Our Only Hope).[1]

---

[1] Taken from 'Vexilla regis prodeunt' (The Royal Banners forward go), a hymn written by the seventh-century poet and priest, Venantius Fortunatus, which, until the 1960s, was sung at the very end of the Good Friday liturgy in the Catholic Church.

Plot

There are no act divisions. Instead the action of the play follows a
continuous progression, which is only interrupted when the main
characters leave the stage briefly to hide in an offstage bedroom.
The setting remains the same throughout, namely the kitchen of a
Swedish manor house belonging to a count. A cooking range, real
utensils and pots and pans on the shelves, and a solid pine kitchen
table and chairs are intended to give the impression of an actual
manor house kitchen. It is Midsummer Eve.

When the action begins, Christine, who is the Count's cook, is
preparing some sautéed kidneys for Jean, the Count's valet: it
later emerges that he is her lover and fiancé. She is also
preparing a foul-smelling abortion potion for Miss Julie's bitch
which is pregnant after mating with the gatekeeper's pug. Miss
Julie is the Count's daughter. She has decided not to accompany
her father on a visit to relatives: instead she has stayed at home to
celebrate Midsummer Eve with the servants.

Jean enters carrying the Count's boots which will need to be
polished before the Count returns home the next day. He
reports, somewhat shamefacedly to Christine, that Miss Julie was
leading the servants' dance with the gamekeeper but insisted on
dancing with him as soon as she saw him. Jean deflects
Christine's irritation at this report by telling her the story of how
Miss Julie broke off her engagement a fortnight ago. Jean saw
her in the stable yard with her fiancé; she was making him jump
over her riding whip until he snatched it from her and broke it
across his knee. This bizarre tale restores Christine's good
humour. She serves Jean one of his favourite meals, the sautéed
kidneys, and brings him a bottle of beer. Instead of the beer, Jean
opens a bottle of the Count's burgundy, which he has removed
from the cellar and has hidden in the drawer of the kitchen table.
As Jean relaxes over his food and wine, his thoughts return to
Miss Julie. He begins by criticising her for demeaning herself by
dancing wildly with her servants; but then he goes too far and

admits that he finds her a magnificent creature. Christine is understandably put out at this and brings Jean to heel by making him promise to dance with her. At that very moment, Miss Julie enters the kitchen.

Initially, she pretends that her errand is to enquire about the abortion potion Christine has prepared for her bitch. All too soon, she spells out the real reason for coming to the kitchen: she wants another dance with Jean. Initially Jean flirts openly with her when she flips him in the face with her perfumed handkerchief. However, he then changes tactics and decides to play hard to get. He suggests that the other servants will soon start talking if she dances twice in succession with the same partner. Miss Julie bridles at this and brushes aside Jean's excuses; she insists on dancing once more with him.

After Jean and Miss Julie have left the stage, Christine is left alone on stage for a scene of 'pantomime', or acting without words. She tidies the dishes, uses a curling-iron to restore some order to her hair, listens to the distant dance music and then, lost in thought, smoothes and folds the perfumed handkerchief that Miss Julie has left behind. Jean enters swiftly, fully aware that Christine is now seriously displeased. His initial tactic is to disparage Miss Julie: he calls her mad for dancing so outrageously. Christine observes that Miss Julie's behaviour is always strange when she has her period coming on. This disparaging remark makes it clear to Jean that he now really has to smooth Christine's ruffled feathers. He puts his arm around her waist and mentions the magic words that she would make a good wife. Just as some domestic harmony is being restored, Miss Julie comes bursting into the kitchen to look for her dancing partner. She covers her obvious embarrassment at finding Christine and Jean at the start of an intimate embrace by ordering him to change out of uniform for this evening of festive celebration. During Jean's brief absence, Miss Julie probes Christine on the nature of her relationship with Jean. Christine defends her status by asserting that she and Jean call themselves engaged. When Miss Julie attempts to belittle this informal arrangement by commenting that she was properly engaged, Christine reminds her sharply that nothing came of her formal engagement.

Jean re-enters dressed in tails; immediately he and Miss Julie engage in a process of flirtatious sparring. While this goes on, Christine falls asleep in her chair. When Miss Julie asks rudely whether Christine snores, Jean replies that she does not; but she talks in her sleep. In saying this deliberately and coolly, Jean reveals that he and Christine regularly sleep together. Apart from making it clear that his relationship with Christine involves physical and sexual commitment, his real purpose is to spell out to Miss Julie that he is a sexually active male who is not interested in playing innocent games of flirtation.

During the pause which follows, Miss Julie acknowledges the fact of Jean's assertive sexuality but quickly recovers her composure. With just a hint of recklessness she continues her seductive game-playing: pulling rank as the mistress of the house, she orders Jean to pour her a drink, to sit with her, to join her in a drink, to drink her health and to kiss her shoe. After Jean has obeyed these various commands which resonate with hidden sexual implications, he warns Miss Julie that they should not go on. Someone might come in and see them, and the servants' tongues are already wagging. Christine is asleep so they are effectively alone.

Somewhat spitefully, Miss Julie responds to this attempt to check her behaviour by trying to wake Christine. Jean intervenes forcefully to stop her: he may be about to betray Christine sexually but he is not prepared to have Miss Julie abuse her. Again, Miss Julie covers any embarrassment by pulling rank: she orders him to come outside with her and to pick some lilacs. Jean repeats the warning he has already given her: if she stoops to become involved with one of her servants, people will simply dismiss her as a fallen woman. His comment encourages Miss Julie to reveal one of her recurrent dreams: namely, that she is on the top of a high pillar and longs to descend to earth but can think of no means of doing so. In contrast, Jean reveals that his dream finds him lying under a tall tree: he wants to climb to the top, view the bright landscape from above and plunder the bird's nest containing golden eggs. These dreams anticipate their respective behaviour patterns during the remainder of the action.

As Jean and Miss Julie are about to leave the kitchen to pick lilacs, Jean pretends to have a speck of dust in his eye. Miss Julie responds readily to this classic seduction technique. As she makes him sit and lean back against her, she even feels his arm muscles and comments admiringly on his strong biceps. Despite Jean's warning that she is playing with fire, she continues to challenge him sexually by comparing him to the biblical figure Joseph who refused to sleep with the wife of his master Potiphar (Genesis 39: 7–15). Egged on by this taunt, Jean makes a physical pass at Miss Julie; she responds by slapping him in the face.

Completely thrown by this contradictory behaviour, Jean responds initially by commenting that he is tired of the game they are playing and that he must return to his duties and clean the Count's boots. But Miss Julie still refuses to back off: she asks Jean if he has ever been in love. This gives Jean a cue to try the next weapon in his armoury of seduction techniques: a sentimental tale that depicts him, as an adolescent, hopelessly in love with Miss Julie. He tells her of the time he crept into the garden toilet pavilion, only to find himself trapped by the arrival of someone coming to use the toilet. Jean escaped by jumping into the toilet and then landing in the excrement pit below. Afterwards he hurtled through the bushes until he saw the young Miss Julie in the rose garden, dressed in a pink dress and white stockings. He hid under a pile of weeds and thought how unfair life was: one of the robbers crucified with Christ might enter paradise, but a poor child like him was not permitted to enter the park to play with the Count's daughter. He claims that he then tried to commit suicide by dashing into the millstream and, when that failed, by lying in an oat-bin surrounded by supposedly poisonous elder branches. This only succeeded in making him ill.

Miss Julie is completely won over by his story-telling. As she melts, Jean switches his tactic back to brutal frankness. He argues that all men and women are the same despite class differences. He implies that she is not as innocent as she claims and is in fact no different from the last woman he slept with. Miss Julie bridles at this assertion of overt sexuality, to which Jean responds by asking permission to go to bed. Yet again, Miss Julie presses on recklessly, asking Jean to row her out on the lake. Jean refuses and treats her deliberately like a thoughtless child who is moving out of her depth. He begs her to leave and go to bed before it is too late. But he can hear the other servants approaching, singing a suggestive song about Miss Julie, and he knows that it is already too late for her to escape. There is only one place they can hide: his bedroom. She makes him promise on his knees that he will be her true and loyal 'friend', and he is only too willing to agree. Shortly after they have hurried to Jean's bedroom, the other servants enter for a scene labelled a 'ballet', which is a scene of animated movement and dance but without any dialogue. Carrying barrels of beer and schnapps, the servants engage in a drunken dance that mimics what is happening offstage: namely, Miss Julie and Jean copulating like a pair of animals. As they stumble away, they repeat their rude song about Miss Julie and her loss of innocence. They leave the kitchen in a state of chaotic disorder.

Miss Julie is the first to re-enter the kitchen. In complete disarray, she attempts to restore some semblance of dignity by powdering her face. Jean enters in an agitated state and continues a conversation they had obviously begun in his bedroom. Now that the unthinkable has happened and that he and Miss Julie have had sex together, and everyone knows or can guess, clearly they will have to flee. Resourceful as ever, Jean suggests a fantasy scenario that he has already envisaged in his dreams: they will flee to Switzerland, to the Italian lakes, and start a luxury hotel together. He can envisage Miss Julie as his front-of-house star, sweetly handing over bills to the guests which Jean will have appropriately inflated. He has even calculated in his dreams how long it will take to reach Lake Como by train from Sweden: a mere three days.

Miss Julie at this stage shows little interest in his scheme: like some abused groupie, she merely wants to be reassured that Jean 'loves' her. She needs to be told that she is not just a cheap whore. In contrast, Jean is now increasingly preoccupied with the social taboos he has transgressed. He has nightmarish visions of the Count returning to discover the full horrors of what has happened and he already begins to cringe. He attempts to bolster his confidence by boasting truculently that he might climb into the aristocracy in some other country like Romania. Miss Julie dismisses his social fantasy as trivial: all that matters to her is that he loves her. Jean refuses to be drawn on this topic. He lights a cigar and asks her in a businesslike manner what she thinks of his project. Briefly she puts aside her demand for emotional reassurance and considers his scheme as a business proposition. As she immediately points out, its key flaw is that it is dependent on the kind of capital neither of them possesses. The alternative, as she herself realises, is for her to stay as Jean's whore in her father's house, which she could not bear.

The next section of dialogue sees Jean taking some delight in diminishing Miss Julie: he obviously did not enjoy the way she brushed aside his project and now intends to hammer home the consequences of being a lackey's whore, while she becomes more and more emotional. He begins by inviting her to share some of the wine he has stolen from her father's cellar. This makes her an accomplice to a sneakthief. He then goes on to tell her that his romantic story about trying to commit suicide for her was just a lie. When he saw her in her pink dress and white stockings, he had the same dirty thoughts as any small boy. With brutal frankness he comments that women always fall for pretty stories. Miss Julie, as Jean intended, is outraged. She orders him to stand when he speaks to her. But this forlorn attempt to pull rank only encourages Jean to diminish her further. To her face he calls her a servant's whore and a lackey's bitch and comments that no girl from his class would behave the way she has. By way of a final insult, he comments that she made his conquest too easy to be exciting.

Again, Jean switches tack. Having humiliated Miss Julie, he claims that he now feels sorry for her. For a while, he reasons with her. She has committed a drunken folly and now wants to convince herself that she loves him: she does not. As he comments that she is too fine for someone like him, he feels his sexual passion re-ignite. Jean is always turned on by a challenge. Miss Julie is wise enough to resist and comments that she detests him as she would a rat, but yet cannot run away from him. At this point in the action, neither of them can think what to do next. Miss Julie's response is to start drinking and to tell Jean the story of her life. Perhaps if Jean knows more about her, he will understand her better. For his part, he warns her not to reveal too much as she must not count on him being a natural ally.

Miss Julie's description of her upbringing goes a long way towards explaining why she is such a confused and neurotic

young woman. It seems that her mother never wanted to marry
her father: nor did her mother want to have children. When Miss
Julie was born, she was dressed in boy's clothes and taught to
behave like a young man. On the estate, the men were made to
perform the women's tasks and vice versa so that the Count
became the laughing-stock of his neighbours. In the end, the
Count took action and put everything back the way it should be.
Meanwhile, her mother became ill: she suffered from convulsions
and often stayed out all night, hiding in the garden. Then there
was a great fire which destroyed the house and all the
outbuildings. The evidence pointed to arson; what was worse was
the fact that the insurance premiums had expired. Miss Julie's
mother suggested that the Count should ask an old friend of hers
for a loan, a brick merchant living near by. He did so and, much
to his surprise, was offered a loan free of interest. Later he learnt
that his wife had started the fire; the brick merchant was her
lover; the loan was money that his wife had hidden from him and
had given to the brick merchant. This was her revenge for the
Count taking charge of the estate. Initially, the Count thought of
shooting himself; instead he spent the next five years making life
thoroughly miserable for his wife. Miss Julie felt sorry for her
father but, because she didn't know the circumstances, sided with
her mother. She also promised her mother that she would never
be a slave to any man.

Greatly bemused by all this, Jean asks whether she hates all
men, including him. She agrees that she does, but when nature
burns, she cannot help herself. Preferably, she would like to shoot
him like an animal. This provokes Jean into suggesting that she
has committed the sin of bestiality with him: in such a case, the
animal is shot and the criminal gets two years' penal servitude.
Once again, however, they reach a point where they do not
know what to do next.

Miss Julie thinks of joint suicide, but Jean will not hear of that.
When she goes on to mention Lake Como, Jean confesses that
Lake Como is less romantic than in his earlier description: it is
always raining and full of young couples who lease houses for six
months and then quarrel and leave after only a few weeks. Next
Jean mocks her ancestry, having reminded her that he did warn
her not to talk too much. As they can think of no solution to their

dilemma, Jean suggests that they should leave things as they are, stay calm and behave as if nothing had happened. Interestingly, it is Miss Julie who points to the flaw in that suggestion. What has happened once could happen again. Jean has to agree and takes fright at the possible consequences. Because of that he orders her to leave at once; he tells her to go to her room, get changed and find some money for her journey. Meekly, and in some confusion, Miss Julie obeys his commands.

Relieved at being alone, Jean opens his notebook and starts making some calculations. At this point, Christine enters dressed for church. She also has Jean's white tie and starched white shirt-front and collar for him to dress for church. Despite all that has happened, he calmly agrees to accompany her. As she puts on his tie and stiff collar, she asks what he has done all night. After he confesses that he has been talking to Miss Julie, Christine notices the wine glasses and immediately jumps to the right conclusions. She is outraged at Miss Julie's behaviour and angry with Jean for abusing the young woman. Immediately, she asserts that she no longer wishes to stay in a house where she cannot respect her employers. She will give in her notice in the autumn and expects Jean to do the same. She astutely seizes the opportunity to remind him that it is time that they set up home together and that he found a stable job, such as a porter or caretaker in a factory, more suitable for a family man. Above all, she wants him to have a job with a pension for his wife and children. Jean is not enamoured of this prospect and can also hear Miss Julie moving around upstairs. He therefore cuts short their conversation and tells Christine to go and get ready for church.

Immediately after Christine's exit, Miss Julie re-enters dressed in travelling clothes. She is also carrying a small birdcage with her pet greenfinch inside. She tells Jean that she has some money but is now too fraught to leave on her own. She pleads with him to come. He agrees as long as they leave at once. Perhaps the thought of slaving away as a caretaker to pay a pension for Christine tips the balance in favour of a romantic exit with Miss Julie. But they must take no luggage: that would give away their intentions. Miss Julie insists on taking her greenfinch: Jean firmly opposes any such notion. Rather than see her harmed by strangers, Miss Julie agrees that Jean should kill the bird. He does so swiftly and ruthlessly, chopping off the bird's head with a kitchen axe. This symbolic deed provokes in Miss Julie an outburst of uncontrolled fury. She spews out her deepest resentments, fears and destructive fantasies in a torrent of verbal violence. She would like to see Jean's brains on a chopping block; she would like to see his whole sex swimming in a sea of blood; she would like to bathe her feet in his guts and eat his heart. She moves on to an apocalyptic vision of the future in which she sees herself telling everything to the police; then her father will have a stroke and die; and the lackey's line will end in an orphanage.

Jean's cynical response to this outburst is cut short by Christine's re-entry. Miss Julie mistakenly assumes that Christine will be a natural ally just because she is a woman. As Miss Julie asks Christine for help, Jean slips out to shave. He can hear what is happening and can be seen in the wings sharpening his razor. He looks on with approval as Miss Julie initially tries to win over Christine with a more detailed version of the fantasy scenario Jean tried on her: a luxury hotel on the shores of Lake Como. However, this time, there will also be a role for Christine. Wisely, Christine says nothing until Miss Julie quite literally talks herself into the ground. At which point Christine only has to ask whether Miss Julie really believes any of her tale. Having crushed Miss Julie, Christine turns on Jean; the two of them then proceed to have a domestic squabble in front of Miss Julie but without taking the slightest notice of her. As they accuse each other of petty theft, Christine has recourse to a simplistic assertion of faith: if she turns to Christ, He will take her sins upon Him. Miss Julie wishes she had Christine's faith. Again Christine crushes her. God will show no forgiveness for the wealthy and for those who have been the first in this world. She sweeps out in self-righteous determination, adding for good measure that she will instruct the groom not to let any of the horses out before the Count returns.

Once again, Jean and Miss Julie are left with the dilemma of what to do. Both of them think of the razor. Miss Julie comments that she does not have the strength to kill herself; nor did her father. She thinks for a moment about who is to blame: her parents or her fiancé for the ideas they gave her; herself? But she has no self. She is too proud to put everything on to Jesus, like Christine does. She will have to carry the blame and face the consequences regardless of whether she is to blame.

At this point, the bell rings twice; Jean changes his coat at once and jumps to the speaking-tube. The Count has returned home. Jean is immediately reduced to the status of a cringing lackey. Miss Julie, in contrast, seems to grow in stature. She needs to save her honour and her father's name, but she does not have the strength on her own to kill herself. She asks Jean to order her to take the razor and cut her throat. As she talks in an ecstasy of anticipation, Jean in blind panic gives her the razor and whispers an order to her. She seeks reassurance about the first having the chance to enter Heaven. Jean cannot give this to her but then he realises that she is now among the last. This gives her some reassurance. Meanwhile, Jean's confidence collapses totally at the thought of the Count ringing the bell and setting in motion a pattern of retribution that will destroy him. When the bell finally does ring again, he first cringes and then orders Miss Julie to leave with the razor in her hand. She walks firmly out to the barn to cut her throat, leaving Jean trapped in a nightmare of his own devising.

Commentary

The Preface

By the time Strindberg completed *Miss Julie* in the summer of 1888, European writers had for some years been fascinated by the notion of scientific determinism. In biology, this concept had first been explored by Charles Darwin in his epoch-making work *The Origin of Species* (1859), which set out to prove that all life was the product of natural selection in an unbroken chain of evolutionary determinism. In aesthetics, determinist ideas were first advanced by the French writer Hippolyte Taine in his *History of English Literature* (1863). Taine described the work of art, not as the creation of romantic genius, but as the product of determining mechanical forces, both physical and social, which act upon the artist. Taine suggested that there were three primordial forces (*la race, le milieu, le moment*) acting upon the artist. The writer reflects or refracts these forces through his individual temperament to produce the work of art. This notion led by extension to the demand that art should in turn concern itself with the genetic, social and environmental forces that determine human behaviour.

Such ideas as these coalesced into the movement known as Naturalism, which became a dominant mode of thinking for writers and theatre practitioners in the 1880s. In 1881 Emile Zola, who was already a well-established novelist and critic, published a collection of essays entitled *Naturalism in the Theatre*. This was widely regarded as a key work for the new Naturalist movement, and it helped to shape the artistic consciousness of playwrights and practitioners all over Europe. Zola demanded that Naturalist stage settings should no longer aim to provide a picturesque framework for stage action, but an illusion of absolute realism. This would permit an audience to see how the behaviour of the characters on stage is determined by the environment in which they live. His key demand for the

Naturalist stage was therefore: 'Environment should determine character'. In addition, décor, costumes and acting should all be integrated into a unified artistic whole so that a convincing illusion of real experience could be communicated on stage. These ideas had a profound impact on Strindberg as he grappled with the challenge of creating a new style of playwriting in the 1880s, beginning with his play *The Father* in 1887. Like Zola, he wanted to strip away the legacy of Baroque and Romantic stage conventions that relied on painted sets, rhetorical styles of acting, and routine patterns of movement and blocking (the placing of actors on stage). He wanted an innovative approach to theatre that would embody the determinist modes of thought expressed in the work of contemporary scientists and aesthetic philosophers. In his Preface to *Miss Julie*, he wrestled with the implications of this revolutionary way of viewing experience. But inevitably, his own temperament gave a highly subjective slant to the way these ideas were reflected and refracted in his account.

In the opening pages of his Preface, Strindberg suggested that the theme of his play, in which a privileged heroine goes under and her family line dies out, should be seen as part of the 'harsh, cynical and heartless drama that life presents'. The process of natural selection, which was predicated upon the notion of survival of the fittest, meant that social change would inevitably bring decline for some and advancement for others. Strindberg felt that this kind of social process should be viewed dispassionately and might even be welcomed by those of a robust temperament. His language at this point seems to foreshadow some of the arguments in favour of ruthless social engineering that would underpin Nazi ideology. He claims that we should welcome the sweeping away of 'decayed and superannuated trees which have too long obstructed the growth of others'. We might even feel relief at their disappearance in much the same way as when an incurable invalid is 'at last allowed to die'. It was precisely these kinds of arguments the Nazis later used to justify the eradication from German culture of any they regarded as degenerate or decayed: Jews, Communists, homosexuals and the mentally retarded. Warming to his theme with some enthusiasm, Strindberg went on to argue that he found the 'joy of life' (a phrase that is mockingly borrowed from Ibsen's *Ghosts*) in 'life's cruel and mighty conflicts'.

Strindberg was not a Nazi. He was a hypersensitive intellectual with a lively imagination who was at this point in his Preface playing deliberately and provocatively with a set of shocking new ideas. There is therefore a lot of deliberate bravado in these opening pages of his Preface. There are also echoes from another philosopher whose work Strindberg had just discovered, namely the German writer Friedrich Nietzsche. Nietzsche was the first nineteenth-century thinker to suggest that the universe was not only absolutely absurd, but that the patterns of absurdity found in the universe recurred endlessly. The first to launch the concept of the Absurd, Nietzsche was also the first to suggest a way of transcending absurdity. In his first (and arguably his only lucid) work, *The Birth of Tragedy out of the Spirit of Music* (1872), Nietzsche gave to art the role of a magic enchantress able to use either sublime or comic techniques both to express life's absurdity and to transcend this absurdity by constructing an alternative aesthetic universe. For Nietzsche it was only as an aesthetic phenomenon that life had any justification. In his subsequent work, Nietzsche went on to describe a breed of supermen who would have the intellectual strength and robustness to contemplate the iron ring of life's recurring absurdity with cynical disdain or sublime equanimity. Clearly, Strindberg had taken all of this to heart and was intent, in his Preface, on conveying the impression of himself as a Nietzschean superman who was capable of viewing the harsh process of life's raw battle for survival with full-bodied enjoyment. While this was deliberate posturing, the aesthetic principle established by Nietzsche assumed a key role in Strindberg's work from this moment onwards: namely that art might be used as a deliberate vehicle not only to address life's absurdity in its themes, but also to transcend absurdity through the formal interplay of line, colour, movement, language and structure. In other words, in a play like *Miss Julie* the darkness of the theme, namely the wanton destruction of a beautiful but weak young woman, is transcended by the formal interplay of the theme with the carefully crafted, aesthetic brilliance of the dialogue, the verbal and visual imagery, the mingling of light and shade in the setting, and the formal structure.

After this bravura opening to his Preface, in which he playfully wove together strands of Naturalist and Nietzschean thought, Strindberg turned to the topic of how he had motivated the behaviour of his characters. The fascinating list of motives explaining Miss Julie's behaviour reads like an extended meditation on Taine's three primordial forces that shape human nature. In the first place, there is *la race*, not the ethnicity of race to which Taine refers but Miss Julie's aristocratic race, which Strindberg sees as a race in decline: 'The passionate character of her mother; the upbringing misguidedly inflicted on her by her father; her own character; and the suggestive effect of her fiancé on her weak and degenerate brain'. Then there is *le milieu*, or the particular environment in which she finds herself: 'the festive atmosphere of Midsummer Night; her father's absence; her menstruation; her association with animals; the intoxicating effect of the dance; the midsummer twilight; the powerfully aphrodisiac influence of the flowers'. Finally, there is *le moment*, the specific moment in time when a new force acts upon these two earlier ones: 'the chance that drove these two people together into a private room – plus of course the passion of the sexually inflamed man'. When one links these three primordial forces together, there is an unbroken band of determinism (or, as Nietzsche might call it, an iron ring of absurdity) that leads to catastrophic consequences.

Strindberg moves on to consider the issue of character. With deft precision, he argues that character originally meant some predominant trait or 'humour' in a person's psyche. This shorthand form of character drawing in the classical and neo-classical theatre was later taken over by middle-class playwrights who showed characters in a fixed manner: they were stupid, brutal, jealous or mean but never unpredictable and complex. From a Naturalist perspective, Strindberg views such an approach to character-drawing as simplistic. In reality, he argues, people are 'split and vacillating, a mixture of the old and new'. Ideas from newspapers and the reported conversations of others have penetrated beyond class barriers. Weaker individuals repeat ideas borrowed or stolen from those who are stronger.

Strindberg next subjects his three characters to some detailed analysis. Miss Julie is dismissed as a half-woman who hates men but would sell herself for power and prestige. He sees her as a tragic type, battling against nature; she is a relic of the old warrior nobility which is now giving way to a new form of intellectual nobility. Even if her father chose not to punish her for her misdemeanour, she would fall victim to the notion of honour which she has inherited from her forebears. Strindberg sees this as a totally disabling flaw, which is bound to make her a victim of natural selection. In contrast, Jean is the ambitious slave who can live without honour and whose lack of disabling moral principles will permit him to found a dynasty. He despises his fellow servants and both admires and hates the upper classes he longs to join. Strindberg describes him as having the brutality of a slave and the indifference of a tyrant. He also sees him as having a dominant position vis-à-vis Miss Julie simply because he is a man. He feels social inferiority, but, as a man, is a sexual aristocrat. Jean's slave mentality finds its fullest expression in his attitude to the Count. However, Strindberg suggests that his respect for the Count derives from the fact that the Count enjoys a social status to which Jean aspires. Christine is dismissed as a female slave, 'bound to her stove and stuffed full of religion and morality, which serve her as both blinkers and scapegoats'.

In these character descriptions, there are further traces of Strindberg's bravado. He writes about the male as the natural sexual aristocrat at a time when he was consumed by jealousy at his actress wife's imagined liaisons with other actors. Equally, some of the dismissive rhetoric he directs against Miss Julie was doubtless fuelled by his own unhappy liaison with his wife, an aristocratic actress married to a man who never forgot that he was the son of a serving woman. Here Strindberg sees his art, not simply as a means of transcending the absurdity of existence, but also as a means of turning life's humiliating defeats into glowing victories.

Finally, Strindberg turns his attention to some of the formal innovations he has pioneered in his play. The dialogue, instead of following a logical linear progression, mirrors the way that the minds of the characters work irregularly. It therefore meanders around; subjects are never fully exhausted; and material from an early stage in the play is revisited and amplified later, in much the same manner as happens in musical composition. The action of the plot is tightly woven and is intended to be performed without any interval. Strindberg explains that he has also broken up the action with monologues, mime and ballet, all of which derive from the practice of ancient theatre. The setting is even more ground-breaking. Instead of a box set, enclosed by three walls and with the imaginary fourth wall between the set and the audience, Strindberg specifies a set with only a rear wall and a table, both at an angle so that characters can be seen in half profile when they sit opposite each other at the table. There are no canvas doors to break the illusion of reality and Strindberg specifies the need for real kitchen utensils rather than pots and pans painted on the canvas sets. He wants to get rid of the footlights, which produce unnatural shadows on the actors' faces, and instead wants to use expressive side lighting. To match this new form of lighting, he demands a natural style of acting. He no longer wants to see actors grouped around the prompter's box (downstage centre), but instead asks for blocking patterns that allow the actors to interact naturally with each other. Scenes should be played wherever the action requires. He would like to see actors without make-up so that subtle reactions can be seen on their faces. He would also like to see small auditoria where audiences are close enough to the actors to see their facial expressions and concentrate on the action without visual distractions.

This final part of the Preface amounts to a practical manifesto for experimental Naturalist theatre. André Antoine, whose Théâtre Libre opened in Paris in 1887, had already implemented some of these ideas in his experimental theatre. But Strindberg's ideas on dialogue, character, setting and lighting were unique. In many ways they also pointed beyond Naturalism to the kind of techniques used in the dream plays and chamber plays that he was to write in later life. For these plays, he was to have his own Intima Teatern in Stockholm, which opened in 1907 with August Falck as its artistic director. The fascinating insights into Strindberg's method of work, revealed in his Preface, suggest that we should approach *Miss Julie*, not simply as a Naturalist tragedy, but as an early dream play conceived, in the spirit of Nietzsche, as a means of transcending the eternally recurring patterns of

absurdity in life with a work of deliberate and exquisitely crafted
aesthetic beauty.

The biographical context

Miss Julie's tragedy is triggered by her arrival in the servants'
kitchen, searching in desperation for somewhere to belong.
Strindberg's insightful portrayal of behaviour motivated by a
sense of displacement may be informed by his own feelings of
social dislocation. His father, Carl Oscar Strindberg, had been a
successful business man, a shipping agent, who even claimed
some aristocratic blood in his ancestry. By the time Strindberg
was born, however, his father had lost his elevated social status:
not only had he suffered the indignity of bankruptcy, but he had
married his mistress, Ulrika Eleonora Norling, who was his
domestic servant. As the child of a professional father and a
proletarian mother, whom he at times dismissed as 'the serving
woman', August Strindberg was intensely aware of the uneven
nature of his 'stock'. It effectively denied him the security of
belonging definitively to any one social class; he felt socially
homeless, and was always uncomfortably conscious of class and
manners. The antagonistic duality of his heritage is
distinguishable in Jean's contempt for the decadent upper classes
and in Julie's loathing of lower-class vulgarity and opportunism.
The all-consuming nature of the play's disdain for both social
strata is symptomatic of the conflicting feelings Strindberg had
about his own class allegiance. The divisive nature of his
upbringing must be viewed as integral in the formation of a man
who was theatrically obsessed with dissonance and conflict. His
very origins lacked unity, making more comprehensible his vision
of life as the playing out of warring factions.

In *Miss Julie* the Count's boots are ominously visible on the set
throughout the action of the play, asserting the determining
effect of the absent father upon the events that unfold. The
omnipotence of the Count's dominating presence is a dramatic
rendition of the manner in which August felt his own life
pervaded by his father's belittling gaze. Because of his
bankruptcy, and because he knew he had married beneath his

station, Carl Oscar Strindberg felt a sense of diminishing social
status and prestige at the time of August's birth. Withdrawing the
'luxury' of all familial warmth, he scrounged for self-esteem by
becoming a domestic tyrant, demanding that everything in the
home be run according to his arbitrary rules. He governed his
household despotically, controlled by the same demons of
inferiority and suspicion that would later hound his son.
Throughout his life, August measured his own weakness against
what he saw as his father's strength, tempering his hatred of the
older man with a cringing fear and respect. In *Creditors* and *Miss
Julie*, this inferiority manifests itself in dramatic form. A male
figure is reduced to a state of impotence because of the link,
direct or indirect, of an older man to the female protagonist: for
Adolf, it is Tekla's first husband, Gustav, and for Jean, Julie's
father, the Count. Viewed from a Freudian perspective, the older
man appears as the shadow of the inescapable Carl Oscar, falling
across Strindberg's texts, punishing the son, by means of
symbolic emasculation, for his incestuous feelings for his mother.
Indeed, Strindberg's childhood followed an almost classical
Oedipal pattern; he adored his mother with a passion he was
later to call 'an incest of the soul'[1] and hated his father as a
powerful and threatening rival. (His first two serious love affairs
with Ina Forstén and Siri von Essen repeated this same Oedipal
pattern: Ina was engaged and Siri married to another man, both
of whom represented the rival father figure.) After his mother's
early death from tuberculosis in 1862, Strindberg constructed a
deified image of her, which induced a relentless yearning for the
purity of the maternal embrace, inside which tumultuous
emotions could be laid to rest. Asked which characteristic he
prized most in woman, shortly before his death, he replied
'motherliness'; Strindberg's worship of the mother in all women
he loved is perhaps why, both in his life and in his plays, sexual
desire, once satisfied, became a profanation. This perverse
attitude to erotic relations is evident in his description of his
feelings towards his first wife Siri von Essen in his
autobiographical work *A Madman's Defence* (1887). So long as
Siri was married to another man and their union remained

---

[1] See Sprigge, p. 54.

'spiritual', Strindberg revered her as a superior being, idealising her aristocratic bearing, her 'white skin' and ethereal purity. As soon as sexual consummation occurred, however, the language he uses to describe her becomes coarse and debased and his virulent accusations of lesbianism, drunkenness, infidelity and prostitution indicate his disgust towards his fallen idol.

It was in 1875 that Strindberg met and fell in love with Siri von Essen, the wife of Baron Carl Gustaf Wrangel, and a member of the Swedish aristocracy in Finland. Strindberg's entanglement in this marriage, first as a friend of both parties and then as Siri's lover, was insidious and collectively scarring. Indeed many interpret the looming figures of Gustav in *Creditors* and the Count in *Miss Julie* as Strindberg's guilt-stricken phobia of the Baron returning to avenge himself. By 1887 August had married Siri, who was drawn away from Wrangel, towards the hope of becoming an actress and living a life of artistic freedom. The charismatic writer appeared to offer Siri the fulfilment of a fantasy existence: a partnership of two artists, unfettered by children and other domestic ties, in which she and her mate could form the centre of a brilliant bohemian coterie. The reality was somewhat less decadent. Siri loved August with an ardour answering his own and, all things considered, was to show uncommon devotion to him; but, as an ambitious woman, she was not designed by temperament to rest content with the part of wife and mother. She craved a career of her own, a career on the stage. Her resulting success, however, put a strain on the marriage, for Strindberg became jealous, suspicious and cruel when she wanted to be more than the submissive maternal ideal he had envisaged. By 1886, his distrust of his wife's loyalty to him, of her sexual morality, and of her suitability to have charge of her children, had become paranoid certainties for him. He ceaselessly suborned his friends to spy upon her, he expressed a desire to hypnotise her, so as to wrest the secrets of her 'infidelities' from her and, climactically, as his paranoia intensified, his behaviour became emotionally violent.

Strindberg's conception of a cataclysmic war between the sexes was undoubtedly shaped by the intensity of the crisis he was experiencing with Siri. It was at this time, inevitably, that his artistic focus shifted from social satire to psychological analysis.

In a manifestation of the intensifying of his obsessive nature, the boundaries of his fictional worlds narrowed. He was fixated by an examination of gender warfare, in which his own immediate problems played the dominant role. Excelling in depicting men and women in a condition of emotional turmoil, his main characters during this period are all frenzied. Indeed there seems to have developed a hysterical reciprocity between fiction and fact, where each fed from and enraged the other. This fills his plays with a potency that derives from their confessional tone; part of Strindberg's modernity is the boldness of his innovative portrayal of raw sexual antagonism. Strindberg's plays were vehicles for his own purgation; while exposing his sexual compulsions, however, they simultaneously explicitly disclosed taboos. Miss Julie's tragedy is that she does not want to sleep tenderly with Jean, does not want to make love with Jean, she just wants to have sexual intercourse. Thus Strindberg reveals that men and women can hate each other and yet be sexually welded together; he knew this because he still was to Siri. The problem was, however, that as much as reality infused his fiction, fiction began to infiltrate his reality, and the line between truth and fantasy grew blurred. This is evident in the overlapping of his biographical accounts of Siri and his fictional sketches of vampire women such as Laura from *The Father* and Tekla from *Creditors*: he began to lose any distinction between his wife and these nightmarish creatures he was conjuring up. For example, in 1887, just as he finished *The Father*, he wrote to his brother in a persona that simulated the Captain's; Siri, in this letter, resembles the demonic Laura, and Strindberg expresses the doubts that destroy the Captain, worrying that his children were not his own. Assuming this blurred perspective of his, in which he and Siri play out their battles within his fiction, one may interpret the sexually lascivious Miss Julie, hunting for 'a bit of rough' to tear her from her social pedestal, as a desecration of his and his aristocratic wife's marriage. His portrayal of a mentally unstable aristocratic woman may be a climactic act of domestic violence against his wife, remoulding her for eternity, via the medium of fiction, as inherently defective and irrational.

Strindberg's plays, and *Miss Julie* is a particular example of this, frequently possess a nightmarish feeling of dark fantasy and suppressed fear. This may in fact be because they are a literary expulsion of the fear that haunted Strindberg's psyche. As Jean cries out in frustration, 'Superstitions, prejudices, which we have been taught from childhood . . .', his anguish is Strindberg's own. Both men are attempting violently to wrest themselves free from the determining influences of their infancy; neither can become truly liberated, however, because they are haunted by ghosts from the past. The boots and bell of the Count serve as a psychological threat, a constant reminder of Jean's servile status, in a parallel manner to the omnipotent presence of Carl Oscar in August's life. Integral to Strindberg's dramatic method is this obsessive repetition of provocative motifs, such as the razor and the boots, in the same manner as they pulsate monotonously through his head. The endless recurrence of these objects, in a style that foreshadows theatrical Expressionism, is indicative of the monomaniacal nature of August Strindberg's mind. Strindberg was intensely aware of the determining effects of upbringing and environment. His own compulsions endowed him with the insight to become the first playwright to depict people locked inescapably into a prison of pre-determined behaviour. As he increasingly explored the artistic potential of his own paranoia, part of his genius was an ability to manipulate his own madness in order to construct creative patterns of expression. For Strindberg, the reality of his own imagination became more substantial than that of the empirical world (a supposition that was undoubtedly integral to his later Inferno crisis); and thus attempting to distinguish where fact has bled into fiction within his writing becomes a complex issue. Strindberg articulated this confusion himself: while writing *The Father*, he did not know if it was 'something I have imagined or if my life was really like this'.[1] What is certain is the fluidity between Strindberg's psyche and his literature: dominant emblems and insecurities flow unhampered from one to the other in a ceaseless stream. The question for the interpreter perhaps becomes how much one values imaginative introspection as a form of truth. To some extent, if one is attempting to comprehend the man, one

---

[1] Letter to his Danish translator, Axel Lundegård, 12 December 1887.

must accept that his perception of his own reality is as insightful as objectivity.

Predictably, August Strindberg, a man who embodied duality, juxtaposed this hysterical subjectivity with the objectivity of scientific analysis. An out-of-control existence was balanced by an obsession with what could be ordered. Aware that his desire for woman as mother made him dependent, he rejected that weakness, attempting to bridle frailty with the mental force of intellectualism. When he first left home in 1867 for Uppsala University it was with the intention of becoming a doctor, and this interest in the empirical sphere of science pervaded his literature. Even after he had abandoned the role of medical student, Strindberg, like the forerunner of literary Naturalism Emile Zola, was fascinated by natural science. He carried out chemical experiments of his own, particularly alchemy, and wrote articles in defence of Darwinian evolution. As he honed his literary skills in his late twenties, his over-ripe imagination was counterbalanced by years of training as a cataloguing expert in Stockholm's Royal Library during the 1870s.

Strindberg's historical context was an epoch in which the grandiose speculative system of religion was being disrupted by the emerging dominance of scientific thought; a development given huge impetus by the publication in 1859 of Darwin's *Origin of Species*. Embittered by the stern and joyless pietism of his childhood (mocked in the religious mindlessness of Christine), Strindberg rebelliously moved towards Darwinistic agnosticism. Indeed as Nietzsche proclaimed God dead and Marx, Darwin and Freud challenged seemingly immutable human laws, *Miss Julie*, provocative in content and innovative in form, reflected the boundary-breaking spirit of its time. Strindberg's intellectual development was as volatile as his emotional life, as if ideologies, after a while, turned as menacing as women and friends; but for the section of his life in which *Miss Julie* was created, he was a Darwinian devotee. From the perspective of this ideology, man must henceforth resign himself to being an animal, with an animal's needs and gratifications. He must submit himself consciously, with what grace he can, to the authority of chemical, biological and psychological laws, and strive, by patient studies of nature, to explore if he cannot control his fate. This was the determined purpose of Zola's Naturalism, to observe humanity objectively via the lens of theatre. In his Preface to *Thérèse Raquin*, where he establishes his Naturalistic intentions, Zola asserts, 'My objective has been, first and foremost, a scientific one.' In the light of the emotional chaos of Strindberg's marriage, Naturalism's self-important air of scientific expertise and precision was for him a relief.

Just after Strindberg had completed *The Father* in 1887, André Antoine, originally an employee of a Parisian gas company but inspired by the Naturalistic novels of Emile Zola, was beginning his mission to purge Parisian theatre of romantic artificiality and replace it with 'real life'. To this end, he hired a room in the Place Pigalle and formed his Théâtre Libre (1887–95), that became mockingly known as 'the theatre of Antoine's back': a taunt fuelled by his dedication to ignoring the audience, and situating them beyond the imaginary fourth wall. Here he presented, by private subscription, foremost works of the Naturalist school that other theatre managers condemned as unperformable. The Théâtre Libre quickly became the rendezvous of the Parisian avant-garde. This was a development after Strindberg's heart, for he too dreamt of a theatre where art and objective experiment were the motives and where the bourgeois and the conventional were barred. Discerning their ideological kinship, Strindberg sent Antoine a copy of *The Father*, and the practitioner was perceptive enough to recognise its merits. Antoine's praise and ideas, alongside the founder of theatrical Naturalism, Emile Zola's, exercised an important influence on Strindberg during this period: not because these ideas were new to him, but because they affirmed and strengthened his existing theatrical ideology. Strindberg's Preface to *Miss Julie* identifiably echoes many of Zola's and Antoine's sentiments, as if he had set out to fulfil their requirements for a Naturalistic playwright. Indeed the Preface to *Miss Julie* may be perceived as an explicit, calculated bid to emphasise the connection between his own writing and Zola's manifesto, in which Zola had cried out, 'Where is the as-yet-unknown author who must make the naturalistic drama?' *Miss Julie* in particular is Strindberg's endeavour to meet Zola's design brief, proving himself to be the new dramatist, an innovator of dramatic form.

Aware that *The Father* and *Miss Julie* were his best theatrical
works to date, and despairing of any conventional director
accepting them for the stage, Strindberg made plans for a
Scandinavian Experimental Theatre modelled on Antoine's
Théâtre Libre. This was to be a showcase for his own plays and
would give Siri a renewed opportunity to employ her acting
talents. Despite the difficulty of his marriage to Siri at this point,
it survived in some form as a working partnership, as they made
practical preparations for the Scandinavian Experimental
Theatre's first season in Copenhagen. Influenced by Antoine's
repertoire of short pieces called *quarts d'heure*, which were based
on violent and sensational themes, Strindberg devised works of
similar intensity: his one-act plays *The Stronger, Pariah* and *Simoom*
and, of course, *Miss Julie*. His first truly Naturalistic play, *Miss
Julie* was to be performed as the company's première and, in a
ghoulish twist to the unhealthy confusion of fiction and reality,
with Siri in its black title role. But on 1 March 1888, the day
before the première of *Miss Julie* at the little Dagmar Theatre was
due to occur, the Danish censor banned the play, effectively
sealing the Scandinavian Experimental Theatre's fate. Having
reached such advanced stages of rehearsal, *Miss Julie* was given
some form of a reprieve, with a private performance before 150
students at the Copenhagen Students' Union. However, with few
resources, and minimal support for his controversial group, it
finished very soon after it had started, simultaneously bringing an
air of finality to the last distinguishable strands of civility in Siri's
and August's marriage.

Despite the termination of his relationship with his theatre
group and with his wife, Strindberg's love affair with Naturalism
continued. It is probable that his intense subjectivity made him
crave the discipline of Naturalism, which served as a defence
against a far too undisciplined imagination. Emile Zola theorised
about the Naturalistic writer, not just as an observer and analyst,
but as a scientific experimenter. Strindberg believed his plays
offered the opportunity to observe humans in a theatrical test
tube. In compliance with the fundamental core of Naturalism
(the use of determinist ideas as the basis for action and
character), Strindberg's Naturalist plays are crammed with the
tenets and discoveries of his epoch. Thus Jean enacts Darwin's

evolutionary theories of natural selection and Christine is a
manifestation of the Marxist economic analysis of society: a
model of the oppressed working class, exuding pietistic prejudice
and an unquestioning respect for class distinctions. Strindberg
perceived himself as a truth seeker and took his role as social
critic with intense seriousness, portraying himself in his poems as
the fireman coming to save the burning house: but 'you prefer to
die in your burning house to being rescued by one, who does not
belong to the fire brigade'. The plethora of 'scientific' ideas and
innovations mentioned in his plays, especially Bernheim's
theories on mind control and Charcot's experiments on hypnosis,
are not used, however, with the neutrality of the unbiased
scientist. It is significant that Strindberg's fascination with
Naturalism begins at a time when his matrimonial difficulties had
grown unbearable; even though, as previously alluded to, it is
unclear whether reality leaked into fiction, or the reverse. Zola's
Naturalism insinuated that social behaviour can be scientifically
examined and proven via the medium of theatre; and so
Strindberg identified Naturalism as a vessel in which to
scientifically 'prove' a motivation for his misogyny. He rounded
up useful scientific theory and manipulated it, to produce his
own propaganda. Darwin's theory of natural selection, for
example, was never intended to explain the behaviour of humans
in the throes of difficult relationships; Strindberg was attempting
to establish as given facts things that were no more than
intellectual constructs. Utilising a variety of modern strains of
thought he developed a rigorously masculine programme:
despising weakness and worshipping the Nietzschean superman,
and regarding life as a nihilistic war to the death between
master–slave, strong–weak, but, most especially man–woman. In
the theatre this self-proclaimed 'scientist' could dissect woman
and expose the rotten nature of her core. What is evident is that
Strindberg's apparent move towards the objective retained his
subjective emphasis and effectively only resulted in him
attempting to distort the scientific to verify his paranoia.

   Strindberg's literary work is one long autobiography. As
previously identified, much of his Modernism derives from the
awareness that he was dipping his pen, quite literally, into his
own unconscious. The persuasiveness of his plays is driven by the

knowledge that their 'truth' is driving him crazy. His emotional nakedness is unswervingly modern. Whether it takes the form of confessional novels, misogynistic short stories, revolutionary verses, anguished letters, theatrical manifestos or plays, Strindberg more than any other playwright writes about himself and the self he continually exposes is split, fissured, divided. Miss Julie is a woman who is at once masculine and feminine, sexual yet repressed, aristocratic yet common in taste. A brief analysis of Strindberg's life reveals that the integral duality of the compelling creature is in fact his own. The struggle in Strindberg's mind between the male and the female, the father and the mother, the aristocrat and the servant, and the scientist and the paranoiac are conflicts which determine the direction of his career, as he projects his personal dualism on to his drama.

Strindberg's Naturalist trilogy

Strindberg's Naturalist trilogy, *The Father* (1887), *Miss Julie* (1888) and *Creditors* (1888), seethe with the ferocity of his fixation on gender warfare. He became convinced that the growth of Modernism, and the women's movement that was integral to it, amounted to an uprising of indomitable Bacchic women. Some of these ideas he found in an article on matriarchy written by the French sociologist Paul Lafargue in 1886 for *La Nouvelle Revue*. Lafargue argued that the existing patriarchal organisation had been preceded by a system of matriarchy. Using evidence from Homer and the *Oresteia*, Lafargue implied that the sexual battle was eternally cyclical, its endless revolutions transcending time and culture. In the wake of the *fin de siècle* faltering of patriarchy therefore, a female uprising seemed to Strindberg inevitable and irresistible. Fuelled by Lafargue's ideas, Strindberg grew obsessive about a glut of vampiric power-hungry women, panting to displace his stability within a patriarchal society. He concurrently taunts and warns men of the dangers of the feminine by creating menacing visions of towering female monsters and the obliteration they instigate. For Strindberg, his Naturalist plays are not solely minute studies of intricate domestic disputes, but symbols, on a grand scale, of the historic vitriolic relationship between man and woman.

The Father is chronologically the opening text in this Naturalistic trilogy and Strindberg's first attempt to meet Emile Zola's demands for objective theatrical performance. *The Father* encapsulates Strindberg's perception of humanity as divided into two halves that cannot be soldered. The opposing forces erupt into cataclysmic battle. 'A tragedy in three acts', it borrows in iconography, fatality and sense of grandeur from the Greek tragedies that, as Lafargue insinuated, prove the inevitability of gender warfare. The Captain perceives his wife not as an individual, but as a figurehead of femininity, her every flaw is characteristic of the female sex: their relationship like 'racial hatred'. Strindberg alludes to this in the Captain's language, which is saturated with paranoid hallucinations of historical ravenous matriarchs. Behind Laura loom the ominous shadows of the biblical Samson's malevolent seductress Delilah, and also Omphale, who curbed Hercules, the epitome of male strength, while he served her as a slave: as he became weaker, she wore his lion's skin and carried around his phallic club. The hysterical exclamations of 'Omphale! Omphale!' dominate the Captain's last speech and prefigure the, almost Expressionistic, linguistic histrionics that Miss Julie explodes with, 'I'd like to see all your sex swimming in a lake of blood – I think I could drink from your skull, I'd like to bathe my feet in your guts, I could eat your heart, roasted!', as she similarly attempts to articulate the enormity of this gender warfare. In a kindred manner to the sunrise at the climax of *Miss Julie*, the Captain's classical references, his elevated speech and his demand for military garb, 'give me my tunic', demonstrate an aggrandisement of his role from defeated party to a martyr for his sex. The effect, however, is inherently deficient, for his sanity and physicality are evidently impotent, as he 'raises himself to spit, but falls back on the couch'. The only semblance of manliness left to the Captain is that of a maimed soldier, surrendering to the enemy. Strindberg's fleeting reversions to the melodramatic conventions of his theatrical epoch (the sunrise in *Miss Julie* and the Captain's overwrought collapse) are false alarms. Although the plays resonate momentarily with sentimentality for the fallen, for Strindberg, the Naturalist and scientist, the only hero is the victor.

As the feminine onslaught demolishes the stronghold of the Captain's identity, this *coup d'état* is demonstrated aesthetically in the stage setting. *The Father* opens in a room littered with the paraphernalia of patriarchy: '*There are weapons on the wall; rifles and game-bags. By the door, clothes-hangers with military tunics on them.*' The Captain, flaunting his props of masculinity, '*with riding boots and spurs*', and the Pastor, puffing on a pipe, seem almost like caricatures of military butch. Theatrically, the rigid walls of this dark, smoke-filled room exude 'containment', evoking the imposing behavioural framework of patriarchal society. Within the microcosm of domesticity this sphere is masculine base-camp; the physical assertion of manliness in this house, from which women can be excluded, or invited in to be dominated. The Captain's ritual in Scene Four of having Laura render her accounts to him, 'Leave the bills there', is merely a technique to induce humiliation. His desperation to impose his masculine authority is instigated by a Strindbergian fear of the female; this paranoia manifests itself in an inability to contemplate equality with Laura, 'If I didn't keep a red-hot iron in front of their noses, they'd claw me to the ground.'

He believes that if he alleviates his enemy's repression then they will strengthen and destroy him. His inferiority complex becomes a self-fulfilling prophecy for Laura responds to this totalitarian regime in kind. As the play progresses, and the rabid women sink their teeth into male flesh, the fortress walls come under siege. Laura paces the drawing room as if it is her own, rifling through the financial documents that earlier epitomised her impotency, '*Laura opens the drawer of the secretaire and takes out some papers*'. Theatrically, one can sense her perusing the masculine headquarters, and infiltrating its dense manliness with feminine cunning. The Captain's identity is inextricably caught up in his ownership of space; by desecrating it with emblems of her occupation, Laura has efficiently destabilised the corporeal location of his self-hood. The fragmentation of his masculinity becomes inevitable. Laura conducts her marital breakdown as if it was a military battle to the death. She is Strindberg's scream of warning to complacent men that warfare has begun and the enemy is well armed.

Laura fluctuates from a brutal figure of machismo, who
confronts the Captain with violence and masculine aggression,
'Woman is your enemy. Love between man and woman is war',
to a maternal giver of tenderness and warmth, '(*approaches him and
lays her hand on his forehead*) What! Man, you're crying!' The
flexibility of Laura's gender identity prefigures the duality of Miss
Julie's concurrent masculine whip wielding and feminine frailty.
The mercurial nature of this third sex's femininity lies at the
heart of Strindberg's accusations of 'corruption' in the Preface to
Miss Julie. His portrayal of Miss Julie's deceitful mother and
Laura infer that a refusal to conform to conventional divisions of
gender affirms an inherent deviousness. If women can evade the
prehistoric barriers of male–female, then there is no confining
them. Thus Laura calculatingly shrouds herself in the protective
veil of femininity to incapacitate attack. In a manifestation of
Strindberg's hyper-paranoia concerning women's inherently evil
nature, Laura resembles the biblical serpent. She entwines herself
suffocatingly around each victim, slithering through the
household, hypnotising her prey into accepting the forbidden
apple of female dominance that she proffers. The imagery of
Laura as a conniving snake, placing subtle suggestion into a
susceptible mind, 'You have dropped them into my ear like
poison', aligns her with Shakespeare's Iago and the Captain's fall
with that of the military hero Othello. There is a certain irony in
this connection, however, for it is Othello's insecurity in his own
masculinity that makes him so susceptible to Iago's perceptive
whisperings. Like Iago, Laura demonstrates the interwoven
nature of seductive charm and immorality, as the Captain
articulates, 'You have a satanic genius for getting what you want.
But that's always the way with people who aren't scrupulous
about what means they use.' Laura upsets the Captain's
intellectual focus and replaces it with a base biological obsession
with his own virility. For an anxious Strindberg, the outcome of
rational man, attempting to adhere to existing structures, is that
he is left bereft by the serpentine, moral fluidity of femininity,
and can only cling to the fragments of his former value system.
Laura's protean nature dominates *The Father*, as her identity
morphs into whatever effigy will most effectively further her
purpose.

Strindberg unleashes in *The Father* an outcry of despair at the
depraved nature of woman; however this anguish is self-defeating,
proffering in itself no resolution. In an act of self-destruction,
reminiscent of the Frankenstein myth, Strindberg absorbed
himself in the erection of a monster that consolidated his
suppressed anxieties; but was then haunted by the creation of this
mutant form of humanity. Laura, the monstrous realisation of his
deepest fears, loomed over him, a literary figure of goading. *Miss
Julie* is the resulting attempt to harness this excessive loathing and
utilise it as a weapon. Strindberg insolently asserts this new-found
bravado in the Preface to *Miss Julie*, 'I find the "joy of life" in life's
cruel and mighty conflicts.' He goes on to command us to
luxuriate in Julie's brutal destruction, 'We shall feel uninhibited
pleasure and relief at seeing our national forests thinned out.'
What appears to be a psychopathically cold and calculated thirst
for female blood, however, is revealed as an impassioned need for
an act of literary vengeance. Jean the valet is Strindberg's fantasy
of raw masculinity, who will avenge the Captain's defeat. By
acting out Strindberg's eroticised ritual humiliation of Julie, Jean
demolishes the myth of Laura's demonic impenetrability. The
'half-woman' can, and will, be destroyed. This play is intended as
a collective catharsis for the emasculated male: they will be
purged of effeminacy by partaking in Jean's indifferent act of
destruction. *The Father* ends with the feeble image of man
physically defeated: Jean is meant to be the phoenix, leaping
from the flames of crumbling manhood. In opposition to the
vision of a masculinity lying limp, bound and straitjacketed by the
rampant energy of Laura, Jean exudes a pulsating physical
dominance. What Strindberg attempts to portray in the lithe
figure of Jean is the potential of sexual magnetism to destroy.
Unlike the Captain, disabled by his elevated intellect and
bourgeois manners, Jean is man devoid of gentility; he is not
inhibited by 'archaic' moral systems but possesses the 'moral
fluidity' manifest in Laura. In this figure of brute manliness,
Strindberg explores whether victory can be won by overthrowing
all instilled civilised behaviour and resorting to a primeval sexual
battle. As Jean 'brings down the axe', savagely hacking the head
from Julie's twittering greenfinch, it is evident that this is
masculinity at its basest. Like Darwinian ape-man, Jean is meant

to be victorious by obeying his carnal instincts. But not even Jean
is quite the man that Strindberg intended. Like the Captain, he
carries within him the seeds of his own weakness and defeat. *Miss
Julie* and *The Father* reek with the blood and sweat of the
battleground. They are messy plays, strewn with bodily fluids and
ugly objects: a razor, a straitjacket, a bloody beheaded bird. A
serene solution to the chaos of gender warfare is irretrievable from
this debris.

Creditors is the resolution of this trilogy, the clinical conclusion
in the wake of the savage battle. All three plays detail humanity's
descent into the mire of mutual destruction. Strindberg shared
with Nietzsche the sense of life as an eternally recurring process
of pain and vitriol; the relationships he showed in his plays are
dramatic representations of entrapment in this interminable
warfare. Strindberg received from Nietzsche, however, a
glimmer of salvation. Nietzsche suggested that when mankind
accepts that there is no God and can willingly embrace the
recurring absurdity of existence, then he will become invincible
and acquire the status of a superman. For the monomaniacal
misogynist Strindberg, it was woman, not the divine, from which
man must overcome his addiction. Following his failed attempt
to batter femininity to death with Jean the axe-wielding ape-
man, *Creditors* is a cold attempt at academic dissection. Thus, in
rejecting the physical, Strindberg appropriates the Nietzschean
state of transcendence to overcome his own eternal hell: gender
warfare. The seductive Tekla is what 'God' was to Nietzsche: a
figure of idolatry who offers momentarily to soothe the emptiness
of men's lives. When Gustav probes Adolf, 'What do you need
her for?', Adolf brokenly confesses, 'What I needed God for
before I became an atheist, something to worship.' Gustav has
suffered the excruciating pain of comprehending that Tekla's
potent femininity cannot endow his life with meaning. His
transcendence of this state of dependence creates an emotionally
immune superman:

> **Tekla**   You are utterly without feeling.
>
> **Gustav**   Utterly.

By emerging from this period of despair or 'existential *angst*',
Gustav holds the psychological steel with which to shatter

inferior minds. While Gustav has weaned himself off this addictive drug, Adolf yearns to remain immersed in Tekla:

Gustav   Bury your need to worship and let some healthier plant grow on its grave. A little honest contempt, for example –

Adolf   I can't live without something to worship –

Gustav   Slave!

Gustav can indulge in this mockery, for he is a slave no longer. Contorting Nietzschean ideas to satisfy his morose pessimism about masculinity, Strindberg has emerged from the vacuous despair of *The Father* and *Miss Julie* with what he believes is a solution: the 'new man' who can destroy the mutated figure of the new woman. This is a colder, crueller figure than Jean, the pulsating lump of virility who flaunts his animal sexual magnetism to lure his victim. Gustav is the psychopath, who partakes in a prolonged stalking of his prey, relishing the thought of the massacre that is to come.

Strindberg's characters seem trapped in their mutually destructive liaisons: in contrast to Ibsen's characters, they seem unable to exercise any free will. The pervasive alchemy of sexuality and violence spawns two opposing urges: simultaneously to savage and yet to escape the Other. The inevitable result of this dichotomy is stasis, as Julie cries out in despair, 'I can't go! I can't stay!' The resulting internal contention is also Strindberg's own. Strindberg's most efficient device to deflate the force of femininity would be to eradicate woman from his text. Instead, he lingers lasciviously upon them, noting voyeuristically Julie's 'pink dress and a pair of white stockings'. The portrayal of 'eternal gender warfare' within these plays may thus be perceived as a facile and pedantic pretence. Strindberg needs the feminine Other to reassert his masculinity. Men require this 'opposite' to maintain their position as dominant upholders of convention. Despite Strindberg's apparent attempt to extinguish the feminine in his texts, it is evident that woman's confrontational presence is essential. She is the subordinated antithesis of rational patriarchy and as such her struggling antagonism validates man's dominance.

The very existence of the Other, however, possesses an inherent threat: woman may rise up from her position as

subjugated deviant and overthrow her master, man. This is the
nightmare that Strindberg sadistically tortures himself with in the
figures of Laura, Miss Julie and Tekla. Thus, as a misogynist with
a feeble grip upon a fragmentary identity, Strindberg lived in
perpetual turmoil. He relied upon the female 'slave' to affirm
masculine mastery but was concurrently tormented by the risk
involved in acknowledging this figure. The self-defeating product
of this duality is an enemy, whom he is entirely reliant upon for
verification of self, and an outcast, whom he must never take his
gaze from, for fear of revolt. Thus, despite his apparent urgency
to discover the route to female demolition, Laura, Miss Julie and
Tekla are arresting presences who command their tragedies. The
dualism of repulsion and attraction that emanates from these
sirens is a product of the pull towards the Other: a pull motivated
by Strindberg's need to affirm his masculinity transmogrifies in
these plays into sexual fixation. The seductive drug of feminine
sexuality lingers tantalisingly, lacing the poisonous gender
warfare with a deadly eroticism. *The Father, Miss Julie* and *Creditors*
trace not only man's desire to destroy that which is Other, but
also his destructive dependency upon and perverse attraction
towards her.

Strindberg has appropriated Schopenhauer's suggestion that
all actions are motivated by erotic intentions: 'Man is concrete
sexual impulse, for his origin is an act of copulation, and the
desire of his desires is an act of copulation, and this impulse alone
perpetuates and holds together the whole of his phenomenal
existence.'[1] Jean and Julie, epitomising the Naturalistic motif of
determined behaviour, are driven inexorably together. Their
environment and language are exhaustively replete with erotic
instigation, each line resonating with a buzzing sexual tension. In
Strindberg's portrayal of man and woman there is a burning heat
that drives them together. Once the desire has been exorcised,
however, these flames linger on, hungering to maim and destroy.
Miss Julie builds in pressure like sexual intercourse itself until the
climactic explosion occurs and all physical urgency evaporates.
The two characters are left staring blankly at a human they hate,

[1] Arthur Schopenhauer, *The World as Will and Representation*, vol. 2 (New York: Dover
Publications, 1966), p. 514.

but are now inextricably tangled up with. For Julie and Jean, lust adds a sheen to the Other which, when smeared away, leaves only a residue of filth and bitterness in the morning. *The Father* demonstrates the inferno when this acridity has become an eternal state of being. Two enemies torturing each other interminably for their momentary submission to the lusts of the flesh, they inhabit endless damnation because of their inability to resist.

In *Miss Julie*, Strindberg explores the seductiveness of debased sexuality but simultaneously the chaos its manifestation induces. If a healthy sexuality propagates vitality, a degenerate eroticism gives birth to depravity. For Strindberg, the act of sexual intercourse is the antithesis of a sacrament; it is a ritual that unleashes the corrupt rather than the holy. The seductiveness of animal physicality haunts this trilogy, for as soon as a character surrenders to it, they simultaneously forgo all supremacy or discipline. In *The Father* Laura poignantly articulates the painful duality of sexual desire: 'Every time your feelings towards me changed, and you approached me as my lover, I felt bashful, and your embrace was an ecstasy followed by pangs of conscience, as though my blood was ashamed.'

There is an innate physical recoil at this joining of her feminine body with its opposite, the masculine, as if she has desecrated her body by forcing it to commune with its adversary. The act of intercourse in these plays is inverted from an act of life-affirming procreation to a catalyst in humanity's debilitation. This ideological pollution of the sexual act is echoed in Strindberg's linguistic corruption of sexual experience. Following Jean's desecration of her body, Julie's language becomes increasingly visceral, as if it were a reflexive linguistic spew, flushing pollution out, 'Oh, I should like to see your blood, your brains, on a chopping block.' The contaminating nature of debased eroticism, having demonically possessed the characters, has now infected even the play's language. Strindberg's characters are compelled towards the transitory 'ecstasy' that Laura describes, ignorant of the interminable personal destruction this momentary pleasure-seeking will incite.

Strindberg is internally plagued by warring factions. A male yearning for sexuality is irreconcilable with an irrepressible sense

of the feminine as annihilative. In a jarring attempt to
'consolidate' this lust and fear Strindberg brings them together
in an image of the consuming female body. Strindberg
prefigures the phallocentric ideas of Lacan and Freud on
woman embodying 'absence' because she possesses no phallus.
In *Creditors* the alluring figure of Tekla is an empty space that
instinctively absorbs identities. Tekla gorges on others until she
is bursting with animation, and they are weak with fatigue. This
motif of the ravenous woman reoccurs in Miss Julie's famished
hunt in the servants' kitchen; yet it is not food she is looking to
consume, but Jean's virile flesh. Gustav, the Nietzschean
superman, having freed himself from his discipleship to this
species of creature, can discern the blood-sucking nature of
Tekla: 'You have taken from me, and what you have taken, you
have consumed, so that you cannot give it back to me.' In
Strindberg's portrayal of woman there is always a sense of filth
underlying apparent purity. In Tekla, for instance, beneath the
superficial beauty is a parasitic leech. Tekla's husband Adolf is
already half 'dead' when Gustav finds him; Tekla has greedily
devoured his soul to feed her own. Gustav attempts to wrest
Adolf's psyche from Tekla's control by spelling out to him the
acts of cannibalism that have occurred, 'The woman has eaten
your soul, your courage, your learning.' Adolf however
epitomises a vampire's victim. He is wan, pale and hovering on
the edge of death and yet desires this ritualistic draining,
'Sometimes I've thought I might find a kind of peace if I was
free, but every time she goes away I long for her.' As Bram
Stoker's compelling Gothic novel *Dracula* suggests, there is an
erogenous carnality to the image of the vampire; the very
allusion to the mingling of blood is a dirty perversion of the
sexual act. *Creditors* throbs with this dichotomy. As the characters
pace around each other warily, eyeing up their prey, there is a
terrifying sense that they may pounce in a spontaneous act of
lust or ferocity. This threatening ritual climaxes in an arresting
tableau, '*Tekla pulls him over to her. He sinks down with his head upon
her knees*', an image mirroring Edvard Munch's painting *The
Vampire* (1889). As Adolf bends down, silently offering his soft
neck to Tekla's 'fangs', the sado-masochistic vision burns with
Strindberg's perception of woman as lascivious monster: the

rabid new woman feeding on the whimpering man. In the icon of the vampire, Strindberg encapsulates his view of the female sex as simultaneously seductive and yet repulsive. Tekla's sexual savagery is hypnotising, mesmerising Adolf into swoons of desire. Tekla as vampire, stabbing phallic teeth into soft skin and thus becoming the penetrator, embodies Strindberg's phobia of the third sex, by appropriating the masculine role of the aggressor.

In the recurring image of woman as vampire, Strindberg portrays a figure who enforces bodily human interaction. Woman is physical, sexual, and messy; she prevents man from retaining a sterile grip upon his own emotion. Strindberg had no desire to feel the pulsing of his own humanity. For Strindberg, the mind was purer than the base object of the human body, and thus he identified the academic as distinctly masculine and the physical as crudely feminine. Yet, despite this disdain for sexuality and corporeality, 'It was my soul that loved this woman and the brutalities of marriage disgusted me',[1] *The Father, Miss Julie* and *Creditors* are as fixated with the physical as they are with the female. Tekla is a woman with immense sexual appetite. She is Adolf's antithesis, swollen with physical vitality, '*Tekla enters, walks straight towards him, and kisses him – friendly, open, gay and charming.*' Humiliated, perhaps, by his own sterile emasculation, Adolf retreats warily from Tekla's sexual excess. Adolf's instinctive withdrawal from Tekla's erotic advances may be an attempt at self-preservation. His body is an object he can physically distinguish, a tangible sign of being alive. To allow Tekla to dominate him erotically is to grant her access into his sole corporeal proof of existence. This is fatal for a man with a slender grasp upon his own identity.

Adolf's awareness of his own physical flaccidity is a Strindbergian self-portrait. Strindberg's biographical work is littered with humiliating confessions of impotence. Strindberg's stubborn focus upon male supremacy, using the intellectual tools of psychic destruction and the Nietzschean superman, is an

[1] A. Strindberg, 'The Occult Diary', in *Inferno and From an Occult Diary* (Penguin, 1988), p. 47.

attempt to remove himself entirely from the sphere of physicality in which he suffers from inadequacy and shame. And yet he is continually undermined by his evident fixation upon the physical. His work does not read as reasoned rationality, but is saturated in visceral re-enactions of his paranoia and insecurities. He aspires to be Gustav, the superman who has risen above his dependence upon women and their sensual offerings. The unconscious preoccupation with the female and the physical in these texts, however, suggests that they still bewitched him. Like Adolf, he is eternally caught in the vampire's grip, addicted to that which destroys him.

The image of masculinity betrayed and imprisoned by victorious woman in these plays encapsulates the evident anxiety of August Strindberg about the force of the feminine. Miss Julie's unwillingness to conform to patriarchal restrictions within the domestic sphere emulates the wider overturning of societal codes of behaviour by the Modernist movement. The correlation between the feminine and Modernism is in their fluidity; both are perceived by rational masculinity as indefinable and thus threatening. Laura and her weapon of 'straitjacket' may be seen as symbolic of the existential despair that was instigated by Modernism's catastrophic boundary-shaking. The image of the Captain imprisoned and impotent inside Laura's straitjacket is a theatrical realisation of Munch's painting *The Scream* (1893), an encapsulation of mankind's despair in this epoch of societal instability. The problematic nature of the feminine in these texts, therefore, might not necessarily be woman herself, but woman as an emblem of Modernism, of the instability of patriarchy and of the decline of accepted structures of thought and belief.

If gender itself is only a symbol of more substantial divisions, why is femininity so viscerally and explicitly demonised throughout Strindberg's Naturalist trilogy? One explanation is that for rational male thinkers, inhabiting an already destabilised epoch, there is something unbearably provocative about the protean nature of femininity. Strindberg, by polarising the feminine, utilised the emblem of woman as scapegoat, thrusting the powerful existential *angst* that pervaded mankind in this period upon her body. Indeed, as we have seen in Freud's theory of the sexual act as symbolic castration, the feminine is innately associated with absence and so the affiliation between her and the threat of 'nothingness' that instigates existential despair is appropriate. Thus Miss Julie's voracious sexual appetite, Laura's menacing appropriation of the Captain's house and identity and Tekla's lascivious absorbance of Adolf's humanity, rather than portraying the threat of a Bacchic uprising of demonic New Women, may in fact be an outcry of despair at life's total absurdity. The apparent fear of the gaping hole of fleshy female sexuality is actually an expression of a deeper despair about an all-consuming void of meaning.

The social context

Strindberg specifies that the action of *Miss Julie* takes place in '*the Count's kitchen on Midsummer Night*'. Much of the action is underpinned by class antagonism and reflects some of the key changes and upheavals that were occurring at the time in Swedish society. Until the mid-nineteenth century, Swedish society had been ruled by its king and a government bureaucracy who consulted, on a formal basis, with representatives of the Four Estates (*Ståndsriksdagen*): nobility, clergy, city elders and farmers. The relationship between the monarch and the Four Estates was in a constant state of flux. At some points, strong monarchs, such as Gustav III in the late eighteenth century, ruled absolutely and used the meetings of the Four Estates as little more than window dressing for their policy announcements. At other times, the First Estate of the Nobility played a far more central role in the government of the country. From the 1830s, however, there were growing calls for a new political order which would replace the meetings of the Four Estates with a proper Parliament (*Riksdagen*) consisting of two chambers: the first unelected chamber to include a large number of aristocrats; the second chamber to be elected and to include many of those, particularly the farmers, who had served in the *Ståndsriksdagen*. This reform was finally passed by all Four Estates in 1865 and the new Parliament was duly inaugurated.

The abolition of the First Estate inevitably brought some loss of status to the old nobility, particularly to the counts and barons who had previously made up the Higher Nobility. The setting up of an elected second chamber dominated by farmers (who were either freeholders or leaseholders renting royal or noble land) confirmed the growing importance of Sweden's prosperous farming community. Sweden had never had a feudal peasantry; its farmers had therefore always enjoyed an independent status. As the farmers consolidated their power base in the latter part of the eighteenth century, they began to enclose common land. The disruption this caused to traditional village life gave rise to growing numbers of impoverished agricultural labourers who were dependent on wealthy farmers or nobility for employment: many also moved away from the countryside to find employment in Sweden's main cities: Gothenburg, Malmö and Stockholm.[1] Others moved abroad in years of particularly harsh deprivation. Inevitably, changes of this magnitude brought opportunity for some but the prospect of starvation and failure for others. All of these shifts and changes in Swedish society form the essential backdrop to the action of *Miss Julie*. Strindberg captures the mood of the period with deft precision. While the old aristocracy is no longer sure of its function or its values, a new underclass of ambitious agricultural labourers is determined to claw its way out of poverty and degradation and exploit every opportunity to better itself. Miss Julie and Jean are archetypal representatives of these two fundamentally contrasting groups.

The stage setting, stage directions and use of stage space

Strindberg's stage setting and his various stage directions make deliberate use of visual signs or *signifiers* to communicate subtextual meaning to an audience. These include the symbolic or iconic meanings associated with objects such as the Count's boots, Jean's razor or Miss Julie's greenfinch; sexual metaphors suggested in features of the manor-house garden such as the tall

[1] Mauricio Rojas, 'The Historical Root of the Swedish Socialist Experiment' (1999), www.stockholm-network.org/pubs/Rojas.PDF

Lombardy poplars or the fountain with a statue of Cupid; the
emotional significance of lighting states, blocking patterns and
movement suggested or specified in the action. These different
visual signifiers need to be recognised and understood by actors
and audience if the rich complexity of subtextual meanings in the
play is to be fully appreciated.

The stage setting is described as follows:

> *The action takes place in the Count's kitchen on Midsummer Night.*
>
> *A large kitchen, the roof and side walls of which are concealed by drapes and
> borders. The rear wall rises at an angle from the left; on it, to the left, are two
> shelves with utensils of copper, iron and pewter. The shelves are lined with
> scalloped paper. Over to the right we can see three-quarters of a big, arched exit
> porch, with twin glass doors, through which can be seen a fountain with a
> statue of Cupid, lilac bushes in bloom, and tall Lombardy poplars. On the left of
> the stage is visible the corner of a big tiled stove, with a section of an overhead
> hood to draw away fumes. To the right, one end of the kitchen table, of white
> pine, with some chairs. The stove is decorated with birch-leaves; the floor is
> strewn with juniper twigs. On the end of the table is a big Japanese spice-jar
> containing flowering lilacs. An ice-box, a scullery table, a sink. Above the door is
> a big old-fashioned bell, of the alarm type. To the left of this emerges a speaking-
> tube.*
>
> **Christine** *is standing at the stove, frying in a pan. She is dressed in a light
> cotton dress, with apron.* **Jean** *enters, dressed in livery and carrying a pair
> of big riding boots, with spurs. He puts them down on the floor where we can see
> them.*

The significance of Midsummer Night is central to the action of
the play. In Sweden, this ancient festival of the summer solstice
with its pagan roots is celebrated the night before the Feast
commemorating the birth of St John the Baptist. Ancient and
more recent traditions combine to make this festival a night of
Bacchic and erotic revelry. There are ring dances around a
maypole; energetic country dances are played by groups of
fiddlers and accordion players; food is laid out on a generous
smörgåsbord; and beer and aquavit flow freely. A wealthy
landowner like the Count would ensure that his servants had a
generous feast, with copious amounts of food and drink and all
the musical entertainment that was expected on such a night. He
might also choose to absent himself from these revelries to avoid
witnessing the worst excesses that could follow from drunken

celebrations which last throughout the night. This is exactly what the Count does, preferring to spend the festival with some of his relations. Miss Julie, who is still smarting from her broken engagement, chooses to stay at home with the servants of the estate rather than face any awkward questions or patronising expressions of sympathy from members of her father's family.

In country communities in Sweden, Midsummer's Eve was regarded as a time when hidden, even devilish forces were at work. Towards the end of the play, Miss Julie refers ruefully to these dark powers when she says, 'Yes, the Devil's been at work tonight.' In the popular imagination, trolls and elves were thought to hide and dance behind the trees. Even the dew was seen to have magic properties. Unmarried maidens were encouraged to pluck seven or nine different kinds of wild flowers during the night and to place these under their pillows. They were then meant to dream of the man they would marry. Jean makes two references to this custom during the course of the action. The first is ironic. In the opening moments of the play, he asks disrespectfully whether the abortion potion Christine is brewing for Miss Julie's pregnant bitch is meant to have the same effect as wild flowers under a pillow: 'Is this some magic brew you ladies are preparing on Midsummer Eve, which will reveal the future and show whom fate has in store for you?' Later, as he and Miss Julie turn to walk out into the park, his comment is more seductive: 'We must sleep with nine midsummer flowers under our pillow tonight, Miss Julie, and our dreams will come true!' There is an oblique suggestion here that perhaps he is the man of Miss Julie's dreams. At midsummer, rooms were decorated with birch branches to celebrate the fertile renewal of nature; and twigs of juniper or other herbs were placed on the floor or the walls to ward off evil spirits, such as trolls, elves and devils.

Strindberg was well aware of these customs and exploits them for their symbolic significance in his stage directions. The birch leaves decorating the stove testify to nature's perennial fertility: and the fertile power of nature is to be witnessed during the action. The juniper twigs strewn on the floor are meant to ward off evil spirits; but they prove less intense in their effect than the forces of nature unleashed during the action. There are further

references to nature's fertile potency in the stage directions. A
large spice-jar is filled with flowering lilacs, while through the
glass doors one can see lilac bushes in bloom. Strindberg himself
draws attention to the aphrodisiac qualities of these flowers in his
Preface. Traditionally the lilac is seen as a symbol of first love.[1]
Beyond the lilac bushes can be seen tall Lombardy poplars: trees
that have a distinctly phallic visual impact. When Jean is seen
silhouetted against them, these tall erect trees are meant to leave
no room for doubt that he is roused and, as Strindberg describes
him, sexually inflamed. Finally, one glimpses in the garden a
fountain with a statue of Cupid the god of Love; the association
of Cupid with cascades of water suggests a process of continuous
love-making. The Roman poet Ovid described Cupid as a
wayward and capricious infant. He shoots his arrows of love in a
completely random manner: as a result, the most unlikely
individuals are attracted to each other, when pierced with the
arrows of erotic desire.

The remaining stage directions are more prosaic and refer
primarily to the Naturalistic aspects of the set. In this play,
however, even the most everyday activities acquire symbolic
overtones. The action takes place 'below stairs', in the servants'
world, which was normally never entered by the aristocratic
mistress of the house. The kitchen is Christine's domain and she
runs it efficiently and effectively. The moment that Miss Julie
enters the kitchen, she is out of her depth and in alien territory.
When the action begins, Christine is standing at the kitchen stove
(almost certainly a wood-burning hearth), frying some kidneys for
Jean's supper. Despite his lowly origins, Jean is a connoisseur of
food, wine and women. Having visited France with the Count
and having worked in Switzerland as a wine waiter, Jean is
perfectly aware that gently sautéed kidneys (with a hint of garlic)
are a great delicacy. Christine is also preparing a foul-smelling
brew for Miss Julie's bitch, Diana (ironically the goddess of
hunting and chastity). The enterprising Diana has succeeded in
becoming pregnant after slipping out to couple with the
gatekeeper's pug. This of course foreshadows the way Miss Julie

---

[1] See A. Stoddard Kull, *Secrets of Flowers* (Brattleboro, VT: Stephen Greene Press,
1969).

herself is to slip down below stairs to couple with Jean. The
noxious brew that Christine is preparing is presumably intended
to produce violent spasms of vomiting in Miss Julie's bitch; the
hope being that the contractions induced by the vomiting will
lead the bitch to abort her foetuses. No such remedy will be
available to Miss Julie after her coupling with Jean.

Real shelves with real kitchen utensils of copper, iron and
pewter underline the fact that this is an actual working kitchen.
There is even a large hood to extract the cooking fumes.
There is an ice-box, a scullery table and a large sink for the
washing-up. As we will see later, any dirty dishes or utensils are
washed and dried immediately. The ice-box permits the luxury
of cold drinks, particularly cold beer. A final touch confirms
that this is a kitchen run by a woman who likes order and
tidiness: the shelves are lined with scalloped paper. Christine
knows how to run her kitchen well and to make it look visually
attractive.

Although the Count and his daughter would never normally
descend below stairs, the Count still has a controlling influence
over the routines of life in the kitchen. His presence is felt by a
large, old-fashioned bell of the alarm type, linked to a speaking-
tube. Whenever he wants anything from the kitchen, all he has to
do is ring the bell and issue his orders through the speaking-tube.
Symbolically, this tube comes to represent his commanding
presence. The same is even truer of his boots. When Jean first
enters the kitchen, he is carrying the Count's large riding boots,
with spurs. He places them on the floor where they remain
visible throughout the action. These boots, with the menacing
threat of the spurs, represent all that Jean aspires to but also the
high-born authority which causes him to cringe. Although the
Count is never seen during the play, his presence is felt in these
physical symbols of his aristocratic status. The boots in particular
almost acquire an Expressionistic life of their own during the
course of the action, as they are cleaned, kicked, mocked, reviled
or revered.

In the opening moments of the action, Christine stands at the
stove in a strong upstage position with her back partially towards
the audience. Jean enters, feeling uneasy and guilty at the time
he has spent away from Christine, dancing and flirting with Miss

Julie. His opening comments are defensive but also have the
intention of re-establishing a bond of solidarity with his fiancée,
'Miss Julie's gone mad again tonight, completely mad!' Jean's
powers of narrative invention soon dissipate any residual
resentment over his lengthy absence that Christine may feel
towards him. As she serves him his sautéed kidneys and he opens
a bottle of the Count's best burgundy, their relaxed domestic
rapport means that he can eat with relish while she continues to
work at her stove. Visually, they operate as an established couple.
Jean sees himself as the quick-witted, dominant figure in their
partnership, but Christine's self-confident body language suggests
a silent strength of character which he respects and values. For a
moment, Jean feels so relaxed with Christine that he even begins
to share with her his growing fascination with Miss Julie whom
he describes as a magnificent creature. It is almost as if Christine
represents for him something of a mother figure who tousles his
hair lovingly and who will forgive him anything because of her
maternal affection for him. Theirs is a solid relationship based on
companionship rather than sexual attraction. Christine wants a
husband who will marry her and take her away from the world
of service and supply her with her own hearth and home. In Jean
she sees someone who will have the wit and the ability to provide
for her. As long as his commitment is real, she is prepared to give
him a loose rein so that he can indulge some of his flights of
fancy. Christine knows how to attract her man (through his
stomach) and then how to keep him.

Their intimate pattern of interaction is soon interrupted by
Miss Julie's unexpected arrival in the kitchen. From the moment
she enters, Miss Julie is uneasy: she should not be in this kitchen
and she knows it. To compensate for her discomfort, she begins
by issuing orders. Christine is told to pour into a bottle the
foul brew she has concocted for Diana, the pregnant bitch;
Jean is then ordered to come and dance a schottische with her.
In contrast to Christine's stillness at the stove, Miss Julie
moves swiftly around the stage like a moth attracted to a flame.
Jean responds, on the one hand, by flirting with her over her
handkerchief, 'Ah! Charming, that smell of violets', and, on
the other, by playing hard to get, 'I wonder if it would be
wise for Miss Julie to dance twice in succession with the

same partner'. The combination of erotic suggestiveness
and masculine indifference proves irresistible. Miss Julie
leaves the kitchen on his arm, like a lamb tripping to the
slaughter.

The stage directions now specify a scene of 'Pantomime' (non-
verbal acting) in which Christine is left alone on stage:

> *This should be played as though the actress were actually alone. When the occasion
> calls for it she should turn her back on the audience. She does not look towards
> them; and must not hasten her movements as though afraid lest they should grow
> impatient.*

> **Christine** *alone. A violin can be faintly heard in the distance, playing a
> schottische.* **Christine** *hums in time with the music; clears up after* **Jean***,
> washes the plate at the sink, dries it and puts it away in a cupboard. Then she
> removes her apron, takes a small mirror from a drawer, lights a candle and
> warms a curling-iron, with which she then crisps her hair over her forehead. Goes
> out into the doorway and listens. Returns to the table. Finds* **Miss Julie***'s
> handkerchief, which the latter has forgotten; picks it up and smells it; then spreads
> it out, as though thinking of something else, stretches it, smooths it, folds it into
> quarters, etc.*

Underlining the Naturalist credentials he has already claimed for
himself in the Preface, Strindberg here specifies that the actress
should follow the practice established by the Naturalist director
André Antoine in his Théâtre Libre in Paris and should turn her
back to the audience when the action requires it. What matters is
that the actress should not 'play' to her audience but should
immerse herself totally in her role and concentrate on the inner
feelings of the character. These feelings are then hinted at in the
succession of small visual gestures specified in the stage
directions. She hums the dance tune played by the distant violin
as she washes up and then puts away Jean's plate. Christine's
love of order dictates that, even when on her own, her first
priority is to ensure that her kitchen is always tidy. But her
humming of the schottische also suggests that she is aware that
Jean is dancing with Miss Julie while she clears. This thought
dictates her next move. She must freshen up her appearance
after so long spent at the stove. The drooping curls on her
forehead need to be refreshed with a curling-iron so that she is
smartened up and ready for the next dance with Jean. Having
restored her wilting curls, she is now ready for Jean's return; but

there is no sign of him. She moves to the door, indicating in visual terms her frustration and perhaps even impatience at Jean's prolonged absence. She may allow him a fairly loose rein, but that is not the same as complete freedom. Practical as ever, she returns to sit and wait at the table where she finds Miss Julie's handkerchief. Mindful of Jean's flirtatious comment when Miss Julie flipped him with her handkerchief, Christine now smells it to catch the delicate smell of violets with which the handkerchief is perfumed. Instinctively, she shows her love of order by smoothing the handkerchief and then folding it into quarters, but her mind is on something else. Her first comment to Jean suggests that in her mind she has in fact resolved to tighten Jean's rein. After his opening comment on Miss Julie's continuing madness, Christine belittles her rival by dismissing Miss Julie's madness as no more than pre-menstrual tension. By implication she insinuates that she is far too sensible and solid to suffer from such an upper-class indisposition. She then goes on to insist on her rights by demanding a dance with Jean. He recognises the irritation in her voice and immediately placates her by saying, 'You'd make a good wife.'

At this very moment of intimacy, the stage directions specify that Miss Julie re-enters and, 'with forced lightness' flutters around Jean whom clearly she has no intention of leaving in peace. Christine is left seething at this renewed intrusion by the young mistress of the house into the kitchen. She bides her time while Jean and Miss Julie flirt in front of her. The moment that Jean steps aside to change his coat, however, she gives vent to her feelings. In a brief but venomous exchange of words, Miss Julie probes whether Jean is engaged to Christine (which suggests that she wishes to know whether Jean is a free agent). Christine responds by belittling Miss Julie's broken engagement, 'Didn't come to anything, though, did it?' The clear implication behind this barbed comment is that Miss Julie, in contrast to Christine, lacks the feminine wit to keep her man.

The stage directions make it clear later that Christine has fallen asleep in her chair. They do not specify the moment when she chooses to sit: this is left to the actress. However, as Miss Julie's jaw drops at Christine's barbed reference to her mistress's failed engagement, it is very likely that Christine adds visual insult to verbal injury by choosing this precise moment to sit down in her chair. Normally, a servant would never presume to sit in her mistress's presence without permission. Jean, whose arm is visible as he changes his coat, has presumably overheard this exchange; he re-enters hastily in his tail-coat to cut short any further verbal sparring between the two women.

What follows is a deliberate ritual of seduction. While he flirts with her, Miss Julie responds by using her superior status to make Jean play erotic games with her. Jean is ordered to kiss her shoe; she feels his biceps as she attempts to remove a supposed speck of dust from his eye; then he is ordered to kiss her hand. Because of her status, she feels secure enough to tease and provoke. She also does her best to make Jean accompany her into the park. There she is mistress; in the kitchen she is not. Jean declines to leave the kitchen where he is on his territory: he may also have calculated that the other servants, having seen him leave the dance with Miss Julie, will come looking for him. That prospect will give him the opportunity he really wants, which is to have sex on his terms with Miss Julie. He does not love her: he despises her. He may admire her body, but feels contempt for her lack of wit. Nor does he want to sleep with her: that would imply spending some time in bed with her. He wants only to dominate her and to deflower her in a savage moment of animal coupling. The process of softening her up is carefully calculated to achieve the desired end: namely, Miss Julie trapped in his bedroom where she can neither cry out for help nor attempt to escape as Jean takes her by force.

Initially, the movement patterns in this scene of seduction revolve around the table, with Miss Julie ordering Jean to sit by her and then kiss her shoe. Next, she orders him to accompany her out into the park. Jean thwarts this move into the park by pretending to have a speck of dust in his eye. Again Miss Julie forces him to sit, but this time establishes physical contact with him, feeling his bulging biceps, as she attempts to remove the speck from his eye. Jean's next move is to make a physical pass at Miss Julie; he tries to grab her waist (and doubtless other parts of her anatomy), as he attempts to kiss her. The final stage of this scene of seduction sees Miss Julie once again seated at Christine's kitchen table while Jean stands over her and tells her romantic

stories from his childhood. Miss Julie is completely won over by
his skills as a *raconteur*, as he spins his verbal web tightly around
her. Finally, she stands as he breaks the spell with brutal
frankness and refers to the last time he slept with a woman.
Shocked and yet still enthralled by him, Miss Julie stands close to
him as she pleads with him to row her out on the lake. Jean
draws back from her yet again as a prelude to the final move: his
invitation to her to come to his bedroom. This is delivered on his
knees: a false gesture of subservience, or even romantic chivalry.
In reality, his thoughts are neither subservient nor romantic. As
Miss Julie hastens out towards his bedroom, Jean hurries after
her, intent on bringing to fruition the brutish act of sadistic
coupling that he has planned all along.

While the two main characters are copulating in Jean's
bedroom, the stage directions specify a 'ballet', which takes place
in the kitchen:

> *The peasants stream in, wearing their best clothes, with flowers in their hats
> and a fiddler at their head. A barrel of beer and a keg of schnapps, decorated with
> greenery are set on a table, glasses are produced, and they drink. They form a ring
> and dance, singing: 'One young girl in a big, dark wood!' When this is finished,
> they go out, singing.*

In his Preface, Strindberg made it clear that he did not want his
ballet 'smudged into a so-called "crowd scene", because crowd
scenes are always badly acted, and a mob of buffoons would seize
the chance to be clever and so destroy the illusion'. In the
Preface he also explains that he has chosen to use the text of a
song he discovered in the countryside near Stockholm. The
words are 'circumlocutory rather than direct'. In the Swedish
text, the words are far more oblique than they are in the
translation used in this volume. But as there is no direct English
equivalent of the folk song used by Strindberg, the translator has
chosen a text that is closer to the more blunt and outspoken
traditions of English folk songs.

The description of the ballet lacks any real physical detail.
Apart from the beer and the aquavit, both of which are freely
drunk, the nature of the dance is not specified. This is left to the
director and the actors playing the roles of the peasants.
Strindberg's use of the word ballet suggests that he envisaged

some form of visual comment on the offstage action, drawing on the disciplined comic traditions of the *commedia dell'arte*. The possibilities are endless. They range from a pair of dancers miming a mock copulation on the table while the others dance around them to the use of the Count's boots as enormous phalluses held by male dancers in pursuit of their female partners during the ring dance. By the time they leave, the peasants have reduced Christine's tidy kitchen to a state of chaos.

The next stage directions describe Miss Julie's re-entry into the kitchen after she has coupled with Jean in his bedroom:

> **Miss Julie** *enters, alone. She sees the chaos in the kitchen, clasps her hands, then takes out a powder puff and powders her face.*

Strindberg's choice of words suggests that for Miss Julie, the state of chaos in the kitchen mirrors very precisely the state of chaos in her mind. After the ritualised game of seduction, Miss Julie finds that in reality she has been subjected to some very brutal sex by her father's valet. She is in every sense of the word undone: her clothes are rumpled and probably torn and stained, her hair is dishevelled, and her make-up ruined. In a forlorn gesture, she tries to repair some of the damage to her self-esteem by powdering her face. Jean enters in a state of agitation. Now that the rush of blood is over and that he is no longer driven by the urge to dominate and penetrate his aristocratic mistress, he simply wants her out of the way. Her continued presence is a threat to his future security.

Initially they stand facing each other as they both try to comprehend just what they have done and what formidable obstacles now cloud their future. While Jean talks expansively and implausibly of them as owners of a hotel on the Italian lakes, he orders Miss Julie to sit: he then lights a cigar for himself. Clearly he now sees himself as a master who can order his sexual plaything to do as he commands. There is, however, plenty of spirit left in Miss Julie. Soon a row flares between them as she discovers that Jean has purloined and is drinking her father's best burgundy. She paces up and down in agitation and orders him to stand in his mistress's presence. His response is crushing, 'Servant's whore, lackey's bitch, shut your mouth and get out of here.' This has the desired effect: Miss Julie crumples visibly,

while Jean stands and enjoys dominating her. There is still a
sado-masochistic momentum to their relationship, which for the
moment he relishes. Roused once again by her collapse, he
attempts to lead her off to the bedroom for more sex. This time,
knowing exactly what it entails, Miss Julie declines vehemently.

For the next part of their interaction together, they sit drinking
her father's burgundy. As she downs far too much of the wine,
Miss Julie makes herself a willing accomplice of Jean the
sneakthief. As he has done earlier in the play, Jean warns her
about the consequences of her actions, knowing full well that she
will take no notice. He points out that if she drinks too much, she
may reveal more of her private secrets than she should, which is
exactly what she does. Jean's aim remains the same here as
earlier: he wants her out of the house and out of his life. Finally
he manages to persuade her to go to her room, to get dressed for
a journey and to find some money (which she does by stealing it
from her father's desk). Significantly, he has to order her to do
this, as she is no longer capable of thinking or acting
independently. This foreshadows events at the end of the play
when Miss Julie is ordered to take even more drastic action.

The stage directions indicate that Jean feels a great relief to be
left on his own again:

> **Jean**, *left alone, heaves a sigh of relief, sits at the table, takes out a notebook and
> pencil, and makes some calculations muttering occasionally to himself. Dumb
> mime, until* **Christine** *enters, dressed for church, with a man's dickey and white
> tie in her hand.*

The visual gesture in which Jean makes calculations in his
notebook is a telling indication of his desire to return to
normality and to pretend that nothing has happened. Christine's
entry with his white bow tie and starched shirt-front serves to
underline the reality of their domestic life together. She not only
feeds him and sleeps with him, but also looks after his laundry
and even knots his white tie for him. Christine can also read him
like a book: she only has to see the two wine glasses on the table
to conclude that Jean has slept with Miss Julie. Astute as ever, she
shows no flicker of jealousy but instead uses Miss Julie's disgrace
as the lever she needs to force Jean to marry her. Jean hears Miss
Julie coming back from upstairs and quickly sends Christine out
to get ready for church.

The stage directions indicate that daybreak has now come and
that the night with all its misdeeds is past:

> *The sun has now risen and is shining on the tops of the trees in the park.*
> *Its beams move gradually until they fall at an angle through the windows.*
> **Jean** *goes to the door and makes a sign.* **Miss Julie** *enters in travelling*
> *clothes with a small birdcage covered with a cloth, which she places on*
> *a chair.*

Later Strindberg came to regret the use of sunlight as an ironic
visual comment on the action (a device borrowed from Ibsen's
Ghosts). In a letter to his publisher Karl Otto Bonniers written on
21 August 1888 he commented that his play *Creditors* was 'even
better than *Miss Julie*, with three characters, a table, two chairs
and no sunrise'. However, the change of lighting seems entirely
justified as a visual device to suggest the harsh reality of the
morning after the night before. Miss Julie is dressed ready for
travelling, but she has brought with her a birdcage containing
her pet greenfinch. For a moment, Jean suggests that he might be
willing to come with her, but he is not prepared to travel with a
pet bird. In a scene, heavy with a symbolism that foreshadows
the final scene, Jean snatches the greenfinch from Miss Julie and
chops off its head. The effect is electrifying: Miss Julie gives vent
to all of her pent-up rage against Jean and his sex in a long,
almost expressionistic tirade. As her anger finally subsides,
Christine re-enters:

> **Christine** *enters, dressed for church, with a prayer-book in her hand.*
> **Miss Julie** *runs towards her and falls into her arms, as though seeking*
> *shelter.*

The attempt by Miss Julie to establish some sort of female
solidarity with Christine by falling into her arms is a gross
miscalculation. Christine has no intention of siding with Miss
Julie against Jean, nor does she intend to relinquish her prior
claim over Jean. While the two women square up to each other
to settle their differences, Jean, in somewhat sheepish
embarrassment, slips out to shave. The visual contrast with the
opening scene of the play could not be more marked. While
Christine stands her ground and shows increasing contempt for
Miss Julie in her words and facial expressions, Miss Julie is
reduced to parroting Jean's harebrained scheme for opening a

hotel on the shores of Lake Como. She no longer gives arrogant orders to Christine, but pleads with her to consider a *ménage à trois* in a far-away foreign country. The stage directions suggest that Jean likes to hear Miss Julie repeat his ideas as if she were an obedient pupil:

> **Jean** *can be seen in the wings right, whetting his razor on a strop which he holds between his teeth and his left hand. He listens contentedly to what is being said, every now and then nodding his approval.*

While Jean has the ambition to better himself, even if his ideas are hopelessly romantic, Christine is a hard-nosed realist whose feet are firmly planted on the ground. As Miss Julie's account of flight into Germany and Italy runs out of steam, Christine completely deflates her with the brutal question, 'Now listen. Do you believe all this?' Yet again, Miss Julie is crushed: she sinks down on to the bench with her head on the table between her hands. While Miss Julie is slumped in this visual position of defeat, Christine denigrates her to Jean as if she were invisible.

After Christine's exit, it is clear to both Jean and Miss Julie that there is no positive solution to the dilemma in which they now find themselves. Both of them are aware of Jean's razor on the kitchen table. As they talk of a possible solution, Miss Julie picks up the razor and gestures with it across her throat: but only to admit that she cannot do the deed. The matter is resolved with the return of the Count. The stage directions state:

> *There are two sharp rings on the bell.* **Miss Julie** *jumps up.* **Jean** *changes his coat. Goes to the speaking-tube, knocks on it, and listens.*

The Count, who has not yet discovered that his desk has been broken open, wants his morning coffee and his boots. Jean only has to hear the bell being rung by the Count and he immediately changes into his livery. Suddenly all his bravado is gone. The Count, simply by his presence, reduces him to the status of a lackey. In this state of panic, he would be quite capable of murdering Miss Julie who, in his view, now has to be urgently disposed of. She spares him the embarrassment by offering to kill herself as long as he commands her to do the deed. Jean gives her the razor and tells her to go out into the barn and (in a whisper) to kill herself with it. As the bell rings a second time, he cringes over the Count's boots and, in blind panic, orders her out. Having degraded Miss Julie both physically and mentally, he now sends her to her death as if she were no more than an impediment to be removed. This final scene moves swiftly to its bleak conclusion. Visually, Jean loses any last vestige of self-control as he clutches the Count's boots to himself in sheer terror. Miss Julie, as if in a trance, walks out into the sunrise to cut her throat.

The relationships

Jean and Christine

Jean's relationship with Christine provides a Naturalistic backdrop to the scenes of sado-masochistic sex played out between Jean and Miss Julie. The scenes between Jean and Christine have the rhythm and feel of everyday reality about them, in marked contrast to the scenes involving Jean and Miss Julie which seem to operate at a level of erotic dream and fantasy. In effect, if not in fact, Jean and Christine are an engaged couple. They are engaged in the sense that they already sleep together and they intend to marry: Christine would never have consented to sleep with Jean without a clear expression of commitment on his part. They both come from the same class of poor agricultural labourers and therefore know what poverty means. They speak essentially the same language and share a similar set of values. Both of them want to better themselves, although Jean's ambitions are more flamboyant and romanticised than Christine's. She wants to have her own home, with a husband who has the wit to provide for her and her children. In an almost Darwinian sense, she has chosen Jean as the ideal father of her children. With his sharp intelligence and his vaulting ambition, combined with her determination, her children will have a formidable set of genes. She is not easily shocked, but there are firm limits to what she will tolerate. For instance, she would never demean herself to flirt with the groom or the pigman; in her view Miss Julie is a fool for sleeping around 'below stairs'. She blames Miss Julie for what has happened, rather than Jean, because Miss Julie has committed the arch sin

of forgetting her place in society. In her view, Jean has done a
wicked deed, but he will come to heel and will still make a good
husband.

Both Jean and Christine enjoy the status that comes from
working at the Count's manor house. Their liveries are provided
by the Count; they have free board and lodging; and they can
afford to dress well when they go to church or appear in public.
They also exploit their positions to earn a little on the side. As
the Count's valet, Jean exercises a wide measure of control over
the other male servants. He also has access to all parts of the
estate, including the stables. His control of the stables means that
he is able to sell off, for personal profit, a percentage of his
lordship's oats. In addition, he helps himself to some of the fine
wines in his lordship's cellars. Meanwhile, Christine who is both
cook and housekeeper takes a percentage of all the groceries and
a rake-off from the butcher. Jean presumably spends his
additional earnings on himself and drinks, rather than saves, the
wine he steals. Christine, on the other hand, is probably saving
the extra percentages she earns for her bottom drawer when she
marries.

Having decided that Jean will make a good husband, Christine
makes sure that his various needs are catered for. She knows
instinctively that the way to a man's heart is through his
stomach, and always ensures that Jean has something tempting
to eat. When she is not too exhausted from her kitchen duties,
she sleeps with him. But the action of the play suggests that this
happens less frequently than Jean would like. She looks after
Jean's laundry and makes sure that he is always provided with
clean clothes. Her technique is essentially to make herself
indispensable to Jean so that he cannot in reality imagine
surviving without her. Her aim is to marry sooner rather than
later and to persuade Jean to find a job as a porter or caretaker
in a factory. Once married, they would not normally be able to
remain in service. It is therefore imperative that Jean finds some
other means to support her and their children with a salary, a
pension and a widow's pension. Throughout their interaction
together, she steers him carefully towards this objective.

Christine lives entirely in the world of daily reality. She speaks
with the conviction of someone who does not believe in

alienation because she has never experienced it. Even religion is used as a tool to bolster her personal set of values. She takes from Christianity its social agenda and believes firmly that, in God's eyes, the lowly are given a high status (because the last shall be first) and the wealthy will never enter the Kingdom of Heaven. But she conveniently ignores those aspects of religion that are less congenial: she never mentions the Ten Commandments and would certainly find it difficult to love Miss Julie (her neighbour) as herself. She goes to church as a social duty but pays little attention to what is said and done there. She has presumably attended church on Midsummer's Day for years but has obviously never grasped the fact that it celebrates the birth and not the execution of John the Baptist.

Jean feels entirely at ease with her, even when she irritates him. A measure of the closeness the two of them share together is conveyed in their use of language. For instance, when cross-questioning Jean about his night spent in Miss Julie's company, Christine can leave crucial points unstated because they both communicate on the same wave-length. All she has to do is get Jean to look her in the eyes and ask, 'Is it possible?' He knows exactly what she is referring to and makes no attempt to defend himself. Normally, in their interaction together, Jean has the upper hand because of his superior status and intelligence. But Christine also has the wit to press home her advantage when Jean is on the defensive. He may not be good enough for Miss Julie, but he is good enough for her and she stresses that it is high time he thought of his responsibility towards her.

Despite Jean's secret dreams of becoming a Romanian count, he is far more likely to marry Christine, his very determined partner, and find a job with a pension to provide for her and the children they will have together. At a Naturalistic level, these two are made for each other; and if he survives the terrifying experience with Miss Julie, Jean will in future find himself kept on a very tight leash. Both Jean and Christine share the same robust instinct for survival that could permit them in future to view Miss Julie, not as a victim, but as the agent of her own self-destruction. However, it is by no means clear at the end of the play that the action will have anything like this Naturalistic outcome. In the closing moments of the play, Jean and Miss Julie

leave behind the world of everyday reality and commit
themselves to a world of sado-masochistic fantasy.

Jean and Miss Julie

Jean the valet represents the figure of masculinity who will
destroy for Strindberg the archetype of 'emancipated' female
whom he despised. In the Preface he describes the new woman
as 'the half-woman [...] synonymous with corruption [. . .] a
poor species'. He commands us to enjoy, or at least find
inevitable, her brutal destruction, comparing it to the clearing of
rotting, diseased trees: 'We shall feel uninhibited pleasure and
relief at seeing our national forests thinned out.' Jean exudes raw
physicality. He enters the stage wielding props of forceful
masculinity like weapons, '*Jean enters, dressed in livery and carrying a
pair of big riding boots, with spurs.*' Julie is compelled towards this
bulging essence of manliness: she wants to touch him, dance with
him and she flutters around him, drawing ominously close, like a
moth to a flame. Jean threatens her repeatedly with the risk of
their proximity, warning her that she may enter into this game
with him but it is not an infantile joke, 'Don't you know it's
dangerous to play with fire?' Jean is acutely aware of the danger
of impulsive sexuality; however Julie seems to have no grip on
reality and no conception of the entrenched social boundaries
she is transgressing. In his allusion to fire Jean articulates the
desire that is quivering between the two of them, capturing the
uncontrollable nature of their hot sensuality. Jean's warning of
both the power of his sexuality and the pain and chaos it may
ignite encapsulates the play's pervasive sense of violent eroticism.

   Strindberg creates in Jean a man who has an urgent animal
physicality; there is a sense of primal strength in his actions, '*Jean
can be seen in the wings right, whetting his razor on a strop which he holds
between his teeth and left hand.*' Teeth bared, Jean resembles a
predatory animal, ready to pounce. He looms over Miss Julie's
and Christine's conversation, scrutinising his territory with an air
of constrained aggression. The brutal alliance of teeth, alluding
to rough, bestial sexual acts, and glinting razor, the weapon that
slits Julie's throat, communicate the lethal combination of
ruthlessness and sexuality at Jean's core. Strindberg asserts in the

play's Preface that Jean epitomises the new nobility. He is a race builder, a man of the future and he seethes with this potent urge to procreate. In an atmosphere of abandonment and decay Jean's energising virility threatens both the audience and Julie with a seductive fascination. He is more, however, than the embodiment of fertility. He is also a man with a thirst for power. Jean is a proto-rapist, he is above all interested in the power and control sex gives him. Strindberg asserts that Jean possesses 'the brutality of a slave and the indifference of a tyrant, he can look at blood without fainting'. Jean manages to maintain this cold element of detachment as he makes each calculated move towards his sexual relationship with Julie. Before he changes his coat, palpably escalating the climate of erotic tension, he says cunningly, 'With your ladyship's permission'. He coerces the victim into deciding her own fate, cruelly placing every shred of responsibility upon her. He is mentally dominating this procedure, embodying Strindberg's belief that all human relationships involve a 'Battle of the Brains'.[1] In a development of Darwin's theories on human evolution, Strindberg presents relationships as a psychological manifestation of 'survival of the fittest'. He believed that as human psyches battle for supremacy in their relationships, the strongest mind triumphs, dominating and manipulating the weaker. As their relationship intensifies, Julie becomes pliable, bending to Jean's increasingly cruel commands, 'Servant's whore, lackey's bitch, shut your mouth and get out of here. You dare to stand there and call me foul?' As Jean's violent obscenity becomes more vehement, Julie absorbs this degradation with an increasing thirst, 'You're right. Hit me, trample on me, I've deserved nothing better.'

Jean, while sexually tempted, is emotionally numb to the charms of Miss Julie; he remains icily aloof throughout her hysterical distress, 'There's only one answer – you must go away. At once. I can't come with you.' Jean is Strindberg's answer to the new woman. He is the new man, physically and mentally tough, possessing the capability to destroy the feminine will in a battle of the mind. In this figure of ultimate masculinity Strindberg has created a brute through whom he can vicariously

[1] The title of Strindberg's essay exploring this subject in *Vivisections*.

explore the sexual fantasy of sado-masochism. Damaged by a sexually confused childhood, Strindberg was incapable of remaining either vulnerable or dominant but swung traumatically from one extreme to the other. Jean, however, the impenetrable Nietzschean superman, possesses the necessary cruelty to embody for Strindberg his fantasy of the strong male sadist.

Jean's sadism could not manifest itself without the presence of a willing masochist and Miss Julie is that figure. She is in a state of internal turmoil. Trained to become an emancipated woman and man-hater by a mother with a confused past, but also encouraged into feminine aristocracy by her nobleman father with his strict codes of honour, Miss Julie is stuck in a bewildering limbo. Taught to despise both femininity and masculinity, she is riddled with self-hatred and utterly lacking in any firm personal sense of identity. Brought up as a boy by her mother, Miss Julie, like Ibsen's Hedda Gabler, has acquired the arrogant aspirations of the men of her class. In a male-dominated society these acquisitions have no use and so they lie dormant, festering inside a frustrated woman. Both Hedda and Miss Julie covet the power of masculinity and so their femininity taunts them. They are innately compelled by it and yet repulsed by its reminder that they are 'other', and cannot inherit the authority of their father. In the burgeoning stages of their interaction Miss Julie is able to command Jean, 'Drink my health, now!', mirroring the Count's ability to do so. However as she succumbs to her sexuality, unavoidably female, she loses the identification with her father (as Hedda does via pregnancy) and forfeits completely her power to control. Miss Julie 'falls' through sex to the condition of a mere woman. Miss Julie's desperate search for identity is dramatically symbolised by her appearance in the servants' kitchen. Her hunt has become so frantic she will search anywhere; she poignantly articulates this sense of selflessness to Jean, 'I have no self. I haven't a thought I didn't get from my father, not an emotion I didn't get from my mother.' Eventually this void inside leads her into the arms of Jean, even if this degrades her to 'a lackey's bitch'; in this position of utter servility, she can at least be sure she can fall no further, which offers her a perverse form of security.

For Miss Julie, utterly bewildered by her lack of any real self, there must be an element of relief in relinquishing control over what seems to be an eternal chaos. By sinking into a role of submission she alleviates herself from her state of unbearable turmoil. Her destiny now lies in Jean's hands; she says to him, 'Order me, and I'll obey you like a dog.' She yearns for the blissful ignorance of the unthinking animal. This innate desire for degradation is communicated vividly by Julie's revelatory dream. Even as she remembers the urgency she felt to debase herself, the overwhelming force of these feelings is evident, 'I can't stay up there and I long to fall, but I don't fall', the pace and repetition of this passage giving it a hysterical desperation. In the image of Miss Julie falling from her pedestal Strindberg prefigures later discoveries by Freud and Jung that dreams are the disclosure of our secret and intimate depths of consciousness. Miss Julie's dream exudes a masochistic compulsion to degrade herself, 'I must come down'; she needs however someone to force her from her state of social elevation, 'I haven't the courage to jump.' This is perhaps why she attaches herself to Jean. She sees in him the sadistic potential that will pull her down. Both Nietzsche, who heavily influenced Strindberg throughout his Naturalistic period, and Freud have suggested that there is an inherent 'slave mentality' in women. Freud connected this directly to the sexual, suggesting that 'masochism is truly feminine'.[1] Freud believed that the risk of pregnancy and dishonour makes sex more dangerous and guilt-ridden for women and so they seek punishment to alleviate their guilt. Miss Julie consciously creates and manipulates this role of abused victim. Jean implores her not to reveal her flaws, 'For your own sake, I beg you!' She is determined to demean herself in front of him, revealing her parents' eccentricities and distasteful past, loading her master with ammunition that he can later pelt her with. To be able to fulfil her masochistic desires, Miss Julie needs a dominant sadist. It is evident from the story of the pathetic fiancé, leaping over her whip, that she has never found anyone who can play this game with her and maintain the desired levels of excitement.

---

[1] Karmen MacKendrick, *Counterpleasures* (New York: University of New York Press, 1999), p. 25.

Perhaps in Jean she at last sees a figure with the required level of brutality.

Jean's dream is the exact opposite: he longs to climb up a high tree and plunder the bird's nest where the golden eggs lie. Miss Julie aids Jean's climb. For her fantasy to come to fruition she must discard their roles of servant and lady and so she bids him '*softly*', a stage direction insinuating an unusual intimacy, to stop using the language of mistress and valet. In *Venus in Furs*, the controversial novel that introduced Strindberg's society to the concept of sado-masochism, Sader-Masoch asserts that 'One can only truly love that which stands above one'. Miss Julie's desperate attempts to rid Jean of his servile status so that he can be the dominant master above her are evident in the episode where she demands that he remove his uniform. She erupts into exclamations of heady girlish excitement when he emerges in black tails and hat, the figure of her lust-fuelled daydreams, '*Très gentil, monsieur Jean! Très gentil!*' By addressing Jean in French Julie builds him up as a man of class and solidifies her bond to him, excluding Christine by elevating Jean beyond her reach. She needs Jean to be lifted up to the level of master so that she can fall to the level of servile subordinate, at last fulfilling her masochistic yearnings.

It is as if for Miss Julie her desire to experience the intensity of life has become stronger than her sense of self-preservation. Thus Miss Julie is innately self-destructive. She embodies the Freudian id, without the controlling presence of the super-ego. She wants sex, alcohol and pain; she wants life to be as dangerous as it can, so she can experience a constant sense of stimulating arousal. In Freud's *The Pleasure Principle* he suggests that the intensity of pleasure we feel is proportional to the quantity of tension released, which explains, to some extent, Miss Julie's desire for pain and danger. The greater the build-up of tension, the greater the pleasure when it is discharged. Through its exploration of sado-masochistic fantasy, in *Miss Julie* there is a sense that we are watching a sexually motivated ritual that has been initiated before; however, until this point, the climax has never been reached. Jean may be regarded as a creation of Miss Julie's psyche, a willing and convenient actor who can be assigned a major role in the drama she is constantly rehearsing and has so

far never finished. In this sado-masochistic ritual there is a
suggestion that the victim desires her fatal end, for she
commands the perpetrator to commit the ultimate sadistic act,
'You know what I ought to will myself to do, but I can't. Will me
to, Jean, order me!' Jean offers Julie the opportunity to break the
eternal cycle of wretched self-abuse and reach the inevitable
culmination. After Jean has instructed her to kill herself, Miss
Julie simply replies, 'Thank you'. This is the end she has been
yearning for, expressed in her craving, as in a Freudian dream,
not just to fall, but to bury herself, 'I should want to burrow my
way deep into the earth.' Death is the ultimate climax for a
masochist, for it achieves the ultimate build-up and then fatal
release of tension. Viewed from this perspective Jean is not the
vilified murderer but her saviour, the first man with the stamina
and nerve to partake in her twisted ritual and maintain his
resolute sadism until its climax has been reached. Her language
becomes hyperbolic and ritualistic, as Miss Julie enters a trance-
like state. At the end of the play, it is as if we have moved into
Julie's dream world: her enforced suicide is the fulfilment of all of
her visions. She speaks her last speech '*in an ecstasy*', as she lives,
at last, the consummation of her masochistic fantasy.

It is evident that Strindberg has created, consciously or not, a
sadist and a masochist in the characters of Jean and Miss Julie. It
is not, however, solely the characters that ooze with this sense of
sexual perversion, but the very essence of the play. This sense of
tainted, somehow distasteful sexuality is all pervasive,
emblemised by Miss Julie's smeared face and dirty fingernails.
What appears superficially to be electric sexual tension is at the
core unnatural and twisted and Strindberg suggests this with
fetishistic symbols and a fleeting reference to bestiality. Miss Julie
has escaped from the repressive aristocratic world of the drawing
room and in doing so she can abandon her aristocratic code of
conduct and indulge in forbidden pleasures. Slumming it in the
kitchen, she has attempted to extricate herself from the
dominating presence of her father's oppressive expectations. To
enter the underworld of the servants' quarters was a reckless
move and that first step makes the next one into Jean's bedroom
distinctly easier. The environment she has submerged herself in
exudes the inevitability of the sado-masochistic relationship that

emerges. The hot, hazy, wild atmosphere of this Midsummer Night almost enforces erotic tension upon the two participants as the characters are enveloped in sexual symbolism. The thrusting phallic image of the 'tall Lombardy poplars' and the entry of the natural world into the kitchen (the birch branches, juniper twigs and lilacs) create an awareness in the opening stage directions that sex is ingrained into every pore of this play. Strindberg even leads the audience through the emotions of sexual intercourse by moulding his play to form the structure of an erotic encounter; it builds with inevitable, unstoppable pace to the sexual climax and then the rush of blood ebbs away leaving a distasteful mess to be cleared up. Strindberg is radical in this play in staging the ugly sound of post-coital recrimination. However the climactic peaks of this perverted sexuality (the sexual coupling, Julie's suicide and the Count's return) all take place offstage. This play is dominated by the unseen. There is something seductive about Strindberg's taunting use of objects, such as the Count's bell, or the razor, which offer us glimpses, like a distorted peep-show, of the explicit acts occurring offstage. They flirtatiously tempt the audience by alluding to the act, without ever satisfying their arousal; it is a form of drawn-out dramatic foreplay. As Jean kisses Miss Julie's ankle there is a sense of indulgence in sexual ritual and sexual display. They relish their own theatricality, cruelly flaunting their erotic tension before Christine, 'She can have another dance with you, can't you, Christine? Won't you lend me Jean?' These slithers of erotic revelation serve as a theatrical striptease, suggesting potently, but never explicitly, the disturbing power games that will manifest themselves during the eventual physical consummation of this sado-masochistic partnership.

However, Jean who partners Miss Julie in this fantasy is not quite the man she imagines. She sees him (and perhaps Strindberg would like us to share this view) as a Nietzschean superman who will stare unflinchingly at life's absurdity and who will send his aristocratic mistress ruthlessly out to commit the masochistic act of self-immolation she desires. Jean is a far more complex character than that. He is the son of an agricultural labourer who has grown up with an enormous social chip on his shoulder. As a young lad playing outside the walls of the Count's

estate, he was painfully aware of the social divide separating him
from the Count and his family. Once, he felt the urge to
overcome these boundaries by engaging in a childish act of
rebellion. He had already previously entered the estate illegally
and, out of curiosity, had fleetingly looked inside the lavishly
decorated and appointed toilet pavilion in the garden: ever
since he had longed to return to experience the full pleasure of
using the pavilion himself. Finally, he plucked up the courage to
do so, but at that very moment one of the Count's guests
approached the pavilion. The only exit Jean could take without
getting caught was the long drop into the pit dug to receive the
piss and excrement of the aristocrats who came to relieve
themselves. Afterwards he fled, covered in shit, and hid under
weeds and nettles. Initially he tells Miss Julie a romantic yarn
about wanting to die when he caught sight of her. Later he
admits that his thoughts, like his physical state, were filthy.
Even as a youngster, he could imagine what he might do to
Miss Julie, embittered as he was by feelings of anger and the
desire for revenge.

As an adult, like so many of the poor, he managed to escape
from Sweden. For a while he worked as a wine waiter in
Switzerland and took great delight in listening to the indiscreet
conversations of wealthy hotel patrons. Now he finds himself
back in Sweden, working on the Count's estate, which as a boy
he had no right to enter. He dreams of climbing out of his class,
and of sweeping away the social alienation he has suffered all his
life. On Midsummer Eve, his opportunity occurs, even if it is
only a sadistic dream. Using sex as a weapon of revenge, he plays
sadistic games with Miss Julie and exploits her like a bitch on
heat. Until they copulate, Miss Julie is a perfect partner for his
sado-masochistic fantasy. She offers him her shoe to kiss: an
obvious erotic fetish. They mention the whip over which her
fiancé had to jump: yet another erotic fetish. Jean then talks of
the garden toilet pavilion and his burning desire to visit it and
'experience the full ecstasy of actually . . .': this too has clear
masturbatory possibilities built into it but the link between auto-
erotic thoughts and excrement is moving into a somewhat
advanced state of fetishised erotic practice. Miss Julie responds to
this notion by dropping the lilac blossom that she was smelling;

but she is not utterly repelled. The erotic game they play together moves towards its inevitable conclusion: a scene of sado-masochistic sex played out deliberately offstage so that the audience is left to supply its own fantasy images of what actually happens.

All through the second half of the play, Jean looks for a convenient way out of what is now a tiresome situation. Repeatedly, Miss Julie is subjected to his withering sadistic scorn: the more she rebels, the more viciously he attacks her verbally. The more she revels in her degradation, however, the more frustrated Jean becomes. He knows only too well that his dream of revenge will be ruined by the return of Miss Julie's father, the Count. Almost as soon as Jean and Miss Julie emerge from his bedroom, he confesses to her, 'I've never met anyone I respected as I do him – I only have to see his gloves on a chair and I feel like a small boy – I only have to hear that bell ring and I jump like a frightened horse – and when I see his boots standing there, so straight and proud, I cringe. (*He kicks the boots.*)' This is no Nietzschean superman, but a grovelling servant who plays out his own set of sado-masochistic, homo-erotic fantasy games with his master. Once again there are erotic fetishes: gloves, a bell, a long speaking-tube and the Count's boots with their spurs. Jean is as besotted with abasing himself before his master and the symbols of his authority as Miss Julie is before him. For Jean, the fantasy of revenge, followed by escape and freedom from alienation, turns into a bad dream. Jean's inevitable final reversion to the role of cringing servant at the end of the play assumes almost metaphysical proportions. Like Miss Julie he becomes the willing victim in a destructive pattern of sado-masochistic interaction; but in his case, there is no obvious exit. He looks and feels trapped in a nightmare of his own devising.

Jean's dream is nauseating. In the end, Miss Julie has to be disposed of, not in triumph but in sheer panic. Even here, Jean's class-consciousness has bitten so deep that he can imagine her behaving nobly and aristocratically, enjoying her masochistic triumph, while he grovels. As Jean disintegrates, Miss Julie has the task of talking him into giving her the razor that will settle the issue. Her masochistic dream is complete at the end: there is even a certain aristocratic purity to it. She escapes from alienation by turning her death into an aesthetically beautiful experience, which overcomes absurdity. In order to find the strength to kill herself, she has taken from Jean his power and vitality and almost sucked out of him, like a vampire, his energy and self-confidence. Jean is now left facing the sordid reality of their post-coital mess in his bedroom and the kitchen. His dream ends in complete defeat. Both sexually and socially he feels degraded. The servant's dream of self-transcendence, using sex as an aggressive means of overcoming rigid class barriers, is shattered. As a young lad he had already dreamt of subjecting Miss Julie to acts of sexual humiliation. In reality, however, she remained a vision of purity in her pink dress and white stockings, while he lay in a flower bed covered in human excrement. The same thing happens again. Miss Julie exits in triumph, given over to an ecstatic vision of purity, to celebrate an aristocratic end to her life; in contrast, Jean grovels on the floor in terror at the thought of confronting the Count. For him, the eternal recurrence of alienation is confirmed yet again and the iron circle of absurdity is complete. At this point the play has moved decisively away from the Naturalist level of everyday reality into an Expressionist landscape of totally subjective, nightmarish experience.

All of Strindberg's plays weave patterns of interaction that attempt to express the agony experienced by people living in a world of alienation. Repeatedly, Strindberg returns to the war of the sexes, where human alienation is most profoundly felt. He shows a ceaseless rhythm of erotic attraction, struggle for power, frenzied coupling, followed by bitter recrimination. This rhythm underpins the whole structure of *Miss Julie*. In addition, the play links sexual with social alienation. The characters are divided from each other both sexually and socially. These divisions are so profound as to be unbridgeable.

Many theatre critics have differentiated the two great Scandinavian Naturalistic playwrights by suggesting that while Ibsen wrestles with larger social issues Strindberg's focus is upon the psychological tension between individuals. It could be argued, however, that Strindberg explores through the analysis of the intimate, in particular the sphere of erotic desires and dreams, the very nature of society. At the time Strindberg was

writing, major thinkers such as Darwin and Nietzsche had
challenged every aspect of a previously stable society and had left
it dramatically shaken, clinging to the remnants of the
intellectual and emotional framework which had once held
everything in place. Jean and Miss Julie may be perceived, in this
context, as modern existential characters; the instability of their
personalities and their urgent need to be defined and controlled
by a dominant force may be Strindberg's comment on the
insecurity of modern man. Strindberg's portrayal of Jean and
Miss Julie's self-induced enslavement foreshadows the existential
angst that later came to obsess Absurdist and Post-modern
theatre. He perceives man's innate need to believe in a higher
force that has control over one's life: this need for someone else
to be ultimately responsible expresses man's inability to accept
what may be, ultimately, the meaninglessness of life. Strindberg
does not analyse, however, the societal confusion of his age by
gazing explicitly at the structure of his society but by focusing
upon the minutiae of human interaction. In the neurotic
insecurity of Jean and Miss Julie, Strindberg foresees the
instability of a society where a dominant collective belief system
has been eradicated. In Miss Julie's and Jean's indulgence in
their acts of sado-masochism he portrays not only a personal
perversion but the collective longing for discipline and security in
a society that has begun to feel inherently unstable.

There is a profound sense of anguish in the bleak ending of the
play. It is not a tragedy, re-asserting man's essential dignity in the
face of an arbitrary fate, but rather an assertion of man's
cowardice, selfishness, and his total isolation from his fellows. In
Strindberg's later plays, following what he called his Inferno
crisis (an almost complete mental and spiritual collapse), the note
of anguish is replaced by the calm of someone who accepts to the
depths of his being that we are indeed isolated and lost creatures
in a totally absurd universe. What emerges is a sense of
compassion for his fellow human beings who all share the same
fate.

Miss Julie on stage

Miss Julie was regarded as a deeply shocking play by Strindberg's
contemporaries. In August 1888, his publisher Bonniers declined
to accept the play for publication on the grounds that it was far
too risky. He also predicted, quite correctly, that Strindberg
would have difficulty in getting the play produced. Strindberg
immediately offered the play to another publisher, Joseph
Seligman, who agreed to publish the work subject to a number of
cuts. Reluctantly Strindberg agreed, and the cuts have remained
in most subsequently published editions of the play.

Given the outraged responses of literary critics when the play
was first published, it is not surprising that theatres throughout
Scandinavia declined to mount a production of the play. (Ibsen's
Ghosts had met a similar fate at the beginning of the 1880s.) In
the autumn of 1888 Strindberg was living in Denmark with his
wife, Siri von Essen, and their children. For some time he had
wanted to found an experimental theatre modelled on Antoine's
Théâtre Libre in Paris. The problems he experienced in finding
a theatre willing to perform *Miss Julie* added to his determination
to launch his own experimental theatre. On 17 November 1888
he placed an advertisement in the Copenhagen newspaper
Politiken in which he announced the formation of the
Scandinavian Experimental Theatre and invited playwrights to
submit short playscripts for performance. He then took out a
lease on the Dagmar Theatre in Copenhagen and planned to
open the first season of the Scandinavian Experimental Theatre
on 2 March 1889 with a double bill consisting of *Miss Julie* and
his newly completed play *Creditors*. The day before the opening
night, the police came to the theatre and announced that the
Danish censor had decided to ban any public performance of
Miss Julie.

In view of the fact that the play was ready to open, Strindberg
decided to find a way around the censor's ban by mounting a
private performance of the play before an invited audience. *Miss
Julie* was duly performed at the Students' Union of Copenhagen
University before a largely male, student audience, although
critics and supporters of the writer were also present.
Strindberg's wife Siri who had not acted for some years, played

the title role and two Danish actors played Jean and Christine:
Viggo Schiwe took the role of Jean and Anna Pio the role of
Christine. Strindberg watched the performance from behind a
half-open door, carefully observing every move and gesture, as
he was convinced that his wife was having an affair with Schiwe.
The reviews of this opening night were mixed. In the Swedish
newspaper, *Dagens Nyheter*, Siri was criticised for playing the role
in far too cold a manner, whereas Schiwe was felt to be too much
a gentleman rather than a servant. Only Anna Pio was described
as giving an acceptable performance.[1] What really impressed the
reviewer was the stage setting:

> The play [. . .] takes place in a kitchen, and completely new décor has
> had to be brought for the evening's performance. To our surprise, it
> resembles a real kitchen. A plate-rack, a kitchen table, a speaking tube
> to the floor above, a big stove with rows of copper pots above it – in
> short, everything is there, presenting the living image of a real
> kitchen.[2]

This first production of *Miss Julie* ran for only two performances.
The next production of the play took place three years later in
Berlin at the Freie Bühne, a Naturalist experimental theatre
established by the director Otto Brahm. *Miss Julie* opened in
Berlin on 3 April 1892, but the production provoked so much
public hostility that the play was only given one performance. A
year later, however, Strindberg achieved the distinction of being
the first modern Swedish dramatist to have a play performed in
Paris: André Antoine opened his production of *Miss Julie* at the
Théâtre Libre on 16 January 1893. The play became an
immediate *succès de scandale*, provoking several negative reviews in
the press, but attracting a lot of attention for the author. He was
interviewed by several newspapers and became famous in Paris
as 'l'ennemi des femmes'.[3]

It took another ten years before further productions of the play
followed, this time in Germany: 1902 in Stuttgart, 1903 in
Hamburg and 1904 in Berlin. The Berlin production was

[1] Ollén (1961), p. 136.
[2] Ibid. Translation quoted from Meyer (1985), p. 215.
[3] Ollén (1961), p. 136.

directed by the young Max Reinhardt who was rapidly
establishing his reputation as a daring and innovative theatre
director and entrepreneur. His production of *Miss Julie* at the
Kleines Theater, with Gertrud Eysoldt as Julie and Hans
Wassermann as Jean, was warmly received by Berlin's theatregoers. At last it seemed as if public taste and sensibility was
beginning to catch up with Strindberg's visionary approach to
modern theatre. Even in Sweden, the public response to the play
was beginning to change. In 1904, a cautious private
performance was given in Uppsala without provoking any
public hostility. Two years later, the young director August
Falck directed a production of the play for the Students' Union
at the University of Lund. This later toured to Gothenburg and
Stockholm. At long last, *Miss Julie* was performed in the
Swedish capital at Folkteatern, with Falck as Jean and Manda
Björling as an elegant Miss Julie. It was an enormous success and
opened the path to Falck's future collaboration with Strindberg
as director of Intima Teatern in Stockholm. This theatre,
dedicated to productions of Strindberg's plays, opened on 26
November 1907. The production of *Miss Julie*, which Falck had
first brought to Folkteatern in Stockholm, became the most
popular piece in the repertoire of Intima Teatern and was
performed in all 134 times (including a private performance for
Bernard Shaw when he visited Stockholm in the summer of
1908).[1]

From this point onwards, *Miss Julie* became Strindberg's most
popular and most frequently performed play. The roll-call of
outstanding directors and actors who have grappled with the
play's complexities is too long to give a full account here. But
some key performances and interpretations can be highlighted.
One of the most gripping performances of *Miss Julie* in the 1920s
was given by the young Elisabeth Bergner at Reinhardt's
Theater in der Josefstadt in Vienna in 1924. She interpreted
Miss Julie as a naive, almost childlike creature. Sigurd Hoel, in
Dagens Nyheter (23 January 1924), wrote warmly of her
performance:

[1] Ibid., p. 138.

> With her slender little figure and her strange face, which above all
> appeared helpless, unprotected, moving, she seemed more a child
> than a woman . . . It was not at all she who seduced the servant, it
> was the summer night, the joy of life, *the powers*, which seduced both of
> them . . . Here was a little child of man who out of ignorance, naivety
> and innocence had made a single *faux pas*.[1]

She reported that audiences were shaken by the ending of the
play and left with tears streaming down their faces.[2] In complete
contrast, the Swedish director Alf Sjöberg directed a production
of the play for Dramaten in Stockholm in 1949 with Inga
Tidblad as Julie and Ulf Palme as Jean, which was earthy,
sensual and shocking. It was also the first production that had all
the dialogue restored that had been cut when the play was
originally published. Sjöberg used this production as the basis for
his film version of the play, with Anita Björck as Miss Julie and
Ulf Palme as Jean, which won joint first prize at the Cannes Film
Festival of 1951. This was not the first success of *Miss Julie* on
screen. A silent film version of the play was made in 1921 by the
German director Felix Basch with the Danish actress Asta
Nielsen cast as a very sensual Miss Julie.[3] The most recent film
version was made by Mike Figgis in 1999, with Saffron Burrows
as Miss Julie and Peter Mullan as Jean. Shot in a vast echoing
manor house kitchen, Figgis brought out the class conflicts
explored in the play but offered no more than an icy and chilled
account of the sexual liaison between Jean and Miss Julie. The
film received very mixed reviews.

The English theatre took some time to come to terms with
Strindberg. Productions of *Miss Julie* in 1912, 1927 and 1935
aroused little interest or enthusiasm among critics and
theatregoers. It was not until 1965 that the first outstanding
production of the play was given in England by the National
Theatre Company at the Chichester Festival. Directed by
Michael Elliott, with Maggie Smith as Miss Julie and Albert
Finney as Jean, this production emphasised the huge social gulf
between an aristocratic woman who is 'pride personified' even at

[1] Törnqvist and Jacobs (1988), p. 243.
[2] Ollén (1961), p. 150.
[3] See Törnqvist and Jacobs (1988), p. 267.

her moment of humiliation and Jean who is played as if 'his servility is inherited'.[1] In 1973, at the very beginning of his theatrical career, Stephen Berkoff created an intriguing version of *Miss Julie,* an interpretation intended to challenge conventional perceptions of the play. Berkoff worked with his newly formed London Theatre Group (1968), who shaped the foundations of his provocative attitude to theatrical performance. Together with actress Maggie Jordan, Berkoff performed an Expressionistic re-working of Strindberg's play, entitled *Miss Julie versus Expressionism.* Berkoff's interpretation of the play was not as subversive or as antithetical to Strindberg's intentions as he may have assumed. By isolating and repeating the images of ringmaster's whip and top hat, the boots, the chopper and razor, the fishnet-clad ankle and the feathers of the destroyed bird, he pulsed sado-masochistic images through the audience's mind. By heightening the sense of sexuality and violence, Berkoff emphasised the pounding heart of the play that lies beneath its cool Naturalistic exterior. It was a production that understood the paranoia and compulsions that are hidden by the appearance of scientific rationality. In 1983 Clare Davidson directed a production for the Lyric Theatre, Hammersmith, with Cheryl Campbell as Miss Julie and Stephen Rea as Jean. Jack Tinker in the *Daily Mail* described Cheryl Cambell's Miss Julie as 'quite the most potent Miss Julie I can remember'. He went on to write, 'To watch Miss Campbell's dizzying downward spiral of self-destruction as she set out to destroy her father's valet is to witness a performance that . . . lies in the realm of minor miracles.' More recently, Patrick Marber's *After Miss Julie* presented a version of Strindberg's play set in England in July 1945, amid celebrations for the Labour Party's post-war election victory. Directed by Michael Grandage, with Richard Coyle as John, Kelly Reilly as Miss Julie and Helen Baxendale as Christine, the production at the Donmar Warehouse in November 2003 received glowing reviews, including one in the *Daily Telegraph*:

> In this electrifying stage version, blazingly directed by Michael Grandage . . . Kelly Reilly brilliantly captures the spoilt hauteur and louche sensuality of Miss Julie . . . Richard Coyle's John matches her

[1] Ibid., p. 249.

every step of the way in this fatal dance of desire, moving from
deference to stinging insults and an eye to the main chance before the
summons of his master's bell reduces him once again to cringing
subservience. Together the pair create an atmosphere of violent and
depraved sexuality that is deeply and disturbingly erotic. An
unforgettable night of white-hot theatrical intensity.[1]

Modern German directors' theatre can normally be relied on to
provide some colourful and highly subjective re-interpretations of
modern classic texts. *Miss Julie* is no exception. Arguably, the
most off-beat in its approach was the 1975 production by the
Berliner Ensemble which presented an Absurdist reading of the
play with Jean dressed in a red clownish sweater and sporting an
enormous erection after the Midsummer dance. After
intercourse, 'the lovers returned with deodorant spouts and
Father Christmas beards in the arm pits'.[2]

Sweden's greatest and most famous theatre and film director,
Ingmar Bergman, has wrestled several times with *Miss Julie*.
Strindberg is one of Bergman's favourite authors and he has
offered a series of outstanding interpretations of Strindberg's
plays throughout his career. Interestingly, however, it was not
until very late in his career as a director (which began in the
1940s) that he turned his attention to *Miss Julie*. It was only in
1981 that he first grappled with *Miss Julie* in a production with
German actors in Munich's Residenztheater: Michael Degen
played Jean and Anne-Marie Kuster played Miss Julie. He
returned to the production several times with different actors in
the main roles and also directed Swedish actors in productions of
the play at Dramaten in Stockholm in 1985 and 1991. In his
reading of the text, Bergman relied on musical rhythms to shape
the emotional design of the production, including pauses,
changes of pace and aria-like monologues. In their book on
Bergman, Lise-Lone and Frederick Marker describe the effect as
follows:

Scenes of explicit and often violent reality were [. . .] infused with an
atmosphere of unreality and dream – one in which Christine's
kitchen-world was transformed, for Julie, into a prison-world of the

[1] www.albemarle-London.com/aftermissjulie.html.
[2] Ibid., p. 254.

> spirit in which she must act out a dreamlike and hopeless struggle to
> exist. Rarely, if ever, has the dreamplay texture inherent in
> Strindberg's 'naturalistic tragedy' been revealed in the theatre with
> such unexpected clarity.[1]

The best of the more recent productions of *Miss Julie* in England,
Germany and Sweden show that the modern theatre has at last
begun to understand the full complexity of Strindberg's play.
Miss Julie is both Naturalistic and, at the same time, a dream
play. The action is triggered by class differences and class
antagonism, but it moves on to trace out sexual power games of
the most intense and subtle complexity. Reality and fantasy are
intertwined in a way that leaves both actors and audience
uncertain as to the precise status of what is transacted. The
decisive events all happen offstage. What is acted out on stage is
a series of ritual power games that are more fantasy than fact and
where the outcome is far from clear. It is this elusive quality,
projecting a shimmering vision set somewhere between dream
and reality, which is captured in the best productions of *Miss
Julie*.

[1] Marker (1992), pp. 105–6.

Further Reading

Collected editions of Strindberg's plays

Strindberg Plays:1–3, trans. and intro. Michael Meyer (London: Methuen, 1989–91). Vol. 1: *The Father, Miss Julie, The Ghost Sonata*. Vol. 2: *The Dance of Death, A Dream Play, The Stronger*. Vol. 3: *Master Olof, Creditors, To Damascus (Part 1)*.

Strindberg Plays: 1–2, trans. and intro. Michael Meyer (London: Secker and Warburg, 1975). Vol 1: *The Father, Miss Julie, Creditors, The Stronger, Playing with Fire, Erik XIV, Storm, The Ghost Sonata*. Vol 2: *To Damascus (Parts 1–3), Easter, Dance of Death (Parts 1–2), The Virgin Bride, A Dream Play*.

Strindberg Plays [The Washington Strindberg], trans. and intro. Walter Johnson (Seattle: University of Washington Press, 1955–83)

Studies of *Miss Julie* in English and Swedish

Törnqvist, Egil and Jacobs, Barry, *Strindberg's* Miss Julie*: A Play and its Transpositions* (Norwich: Norvik Press, 1988)

Lagerroth, Ulla-Britta and Lindström, Göran (eds), *Perspektiv på Fröken Julie* (Stockholm: Rabén & Sjögren, 1972)

Biographical studies of Strindberg

Lamm, Martin, *August Strindberg* (New York: Bloom, 1971)

Meyer, Michael, *Strindberg: A Biography* (London: Secker & Warburg, 1985)

Mortenson, Brita and Downs, Brian, *Strindberg, an Introduction to his Life and Work* (Cambridge: CUP, 1949)

Robinson, Michael, *Strindberg and Autobiography: Writing and Reading a Life* (Norwich: Norvik Press, 1986)

Sprigge, Elizabeth, *The Strange Life of August Strindberg* (London: Hamish Hamilton, 1949)

Critical approaches to Strindberg

Madsen, Børge Gedsø: *Strindberg's Naturalistic Theatre, its Relation to French Naturalism* [1962] (New York: Russell & Russell, 1973)
Morgan, Margery, *August Strindberg* (Basingstoke: Macmillan, 1985)
Ollén, Gunnar, *Strindberg* (New York: Ungar, 1972)
Reinert, Otto (ed.), *Strindberg: A Collection of Critical Essays* (Englewood Cliffs: Prentice-Hall, 1971)
Sprinchorn, Evert, *Strindberg as Dramatist* (New Haven: Yale University Press, 1982)
Steene, Birgitta, *August Strindberg: An Introduction to his Major Works* (Stockholm: Almqvist & Wiksell, 1982)
Törnqvist, Egil, *Strindbergian Drama: Themes and Structure* (Stockholm: Almqvist & Wiksell, 1982)
Valency, Maurice, *The Flower and the Castle* (London: Macmillan, 1963)
Williams, Raymond, *Modern Tragedy* (London: Chatto & Windus, 1966)

Strindberg and the theatre

Innes, Christopher, *A Sourcebook on Naturalist Theatre* (London: Routledge, 2000)
Marker, Frederick and Lise-Lone, *The Scandinavian Theatre: A Short History* (Oxford: Blackwell, 1975)
——, *Ingmar Bergman. A Life in the Theatre* (Cambridge: CUP 1992)
——, *A History of Scandinavian Theatre* (Cambridge: CUP, 1996)
——, *Strindberg and Modernist Theatre: Post-Inferno Drama on the Stage* (Cambridge: CUP, 2002)
Martin, Jacqueline (ed.), 'Strindberg in Performance' in *Nordic Theatre Studies*, vol. 6, 1–2 (Oxford: OUP in association with the International Federation for Theatre Research, 1993)
Ollén, Gunnar, *Strindbergs dramatik* (Stockholm: Sveriges Radio, 1961)

Miss Julie

A NATURALISTIC TRAGEDY
(1888)

translated by Michael Meyer

Strindberg's Preface to *Miss Julie*

The theatre, and indeed art in general, has long seemed to me a
Biblia pauperum, a Bible in pictures for the benefit of the illiterate;
with the dramatist as a lay preacher hawking contemporary ideas
in a popular form, popular enough for the middle classes, who
comprise the bulk of playgoers, to be able to grasp without too
much effort what the minority is arguing about. The theatre has
always been a primary school for the young, the semi-educated,
and women, all of whom retain the humble faculty of being able
to deceive themselves and let themselves be deceived – in other
words, to accept the illusion, and react to the suggestion, of the
author. Nowadays the primitive process of intuition is giving way
to reflection, investigation and analysis, and I feel that the
theatre, like religion, is on the way to being discarded as a dying
form which we lack the necessary conditions to enjoy. This
hypothesis is evidenced by the theatrical crisis now dominating
the whole of Europe; and, not least, by the fact that in those
cultural strongholds which have nurtured the greatest thinkers of
our age, namely England and Germany, the art of writing plays
is, like most of the other fine arts, dead.

In other countries, men have tried to create a new drama by
pouring new ideas into the old forms. But this has failed, partly
because the new thinkers have not yet had time to become
popularised and thus educate the public to understand the issues
involved; partly because polemical differences have so inflamed
emotions that dispassionate appreciation has become impossible
– the cheers and whistles of the majority exercise a pressure that
upsets one's instinctive reaction – and partly also because we
have not succeeded in adapting the old form to the new content,
so that the new wine has burst the old bottles.

In my previous plays, I have not tried to do anything new – for
that one can never do – but merely to modernise the form so as
to meet the demands which I supposed that the new men and
women of today would make of this art. To this end I chose, or
let myself be caught up by, a theme which may be said to lie

outside current party conflicts. For the problem of social ascent and decline, of higher or lower, better or worse, man or woman, is, has been and will be of permanent interest. When I took this theme from an actual incident which I heard about some years ago, and which at the time made a deep impression on me, it seemed to me suitable matter for tragedy; for it is still tragic to see one on whom fortune has smiled go under, much more to see a line die out. But the time may come when we shall have become so developed and enlightened that we shall be able to observe with indifference the harsh, cynical and heartless drama that life presents – when we shall have discarded those inferior and unreliable thought-mechanisms called feelings, which will become superfluous and harmful once our powers of judgement reach maturity. The fact that the heroine arouses our sympathy is merely due to our weakness in not being able to resist a feeling of fear lest the same fate should befall us. Even so, the hyper-sensitive spectator may possibly even feel that sympathy is not enough, while the politically-minded will doubtless demand positive measures to remedy the evil – some kind of 'programme'. But there is no such thing as absolute evil, since the death of a family is good luck for some other family that will be able to take its place, and social change constitutes one of the main pleasures of life, happiness being dependent on comparison. As for the political planner, who wishes to remedy the regrettable fact that the bird of prey eats the dove, and the louse eats the bird of prey, I would ask him 'Why should this state of affairs be remedied?' Life is not so foolishly and mathematically arranged that the great always devour the small. It happens equally often that a bee kills a lion, or at any rate drives it mad.

If my tragedy makes a tragic impression on people, they have only themselves to blame. When we become as strong as the first French revolutionaries, we shall feel uninhibited pleasure and relief at seeing our national forests thinned out by the removal of decayed and superannuated trees which have too long obstructed the growth of others with an equal right to live and fertilise their age – a relief such as one feels when one sees an incurable invalid at last allowed to die.

Recently, people complained of my tragedy *The Father* that it was too tragic – as though tragedies ought to be jolly. One hears

pretentious talk about 'the joy of life',[1] and theatrical managers
feverishly commission farces, as though joy consisted in behaving
idiotically and portraying the world as though it were peopled by
lunatics with an insatiable passion for dancing. I find 'the joy of
life' in life's cruel and mighty conflicts; I delight in knowledge
and discovery. And that is why I have chosen a case that is
unusual but from which one can learn much – an exception, if
you like, but an important exception which proves the rule –
though I dare say it will offend those people who love only what
is commonplace. Another thing that will offend simple souls is
the fact that the motivation of my play is not simple, and that life
is seen from more than one viewpoint. An incident in real life
(and this is quite a new discovery!) is usually the outcome of a
whole series of deep-buried motives, but the spectator commonly
settles for the one that he finds easiest to understand, or that he
finds most flattering to his powers of judgement. Someone
commits suicide. 'Bad business!', says the business man.
'Unrequited love!', say the ladies. 'Bodily illness!', says the
invalid. 'Shattered hopes!', says the man who is a failure. But it
may be that the motive lay quite elsewhere, or nowhere, and that
the dead man concealed his true motive by suggesting another
more likely to do credit to his memory!

I have suggested many possible motivations for Miss Julie's
unhappy fate. The passionate character of her mother; the
upbringing misguidedly inflicted on her by her father; her own
character; and the suggestive effect of her fiancé upon her weak
and degenerate brain. Also, more immediately, the festive
atmosphere of Midsummer Night; her father's absence; her
menstruation; her association with animals; the intoxicating
effect of the dance; the midsummer twilight; the powerfully
aphrodisiac influence of the flowers; and, finally, the chance that
drove these two people together into a private room – plus of
course the passion of the sexually inflamed man.

I have therefore not suggested that the motivation was purely
physiological, nor that it was exclusively psychological. I have not
attributed her fate solely to her heritage, nor thrown the entire

[1] 'The joy of life' (*livsglæde*) is a key-phrase in Ibsen's *Ghosts*, published seven years
before Strindberg wrote *Miss Julie*.

blame on to her menstruation, or her lack of morals. I have not set out to preach morality. This, in the absence of a priest, I have left to a cook.

This multiplicity of motives is, I like to think, typical of our times. And if others have done this before me, then I congratulate myself in not being alone in my belief in these 'paradoxes' (the word always used to describe new discoveries).

As regards characterisation, I have made my protagonists somewhat lacking in 'character', for the following reasons:

The word 'character' has, over the years, frequently changed its meaning. Originally it meant the dominant feature in a person's psyche, and was synonymous with temperament. Then it became the middle-class euphemism for an automaton; so that an individual who had stopped developing, or who had moulded himself to a fixed role in life – in other words, stopped growing – came to be called a 'character' – whereas the man who goes on developing, the skilful navigator of life's river, who does not sail with a fixed sheet but rides before the wind to luff again, was stigmatised as 'characterless' (in, of course, a derogatory sense) because he was too difficult to catch, classify and keep tabs on. This *bourgeois* conception of the immutability of the soul became transferred to the stage, which had always been *bourgeois*-dominated. A character, there, became a man fixed in a mould, who always appeared drunk, or comic, or pathetic, and to establish whom it was only necessary to equip with some physical defect, such as a club-foot, a wooden leg or a red nose, or else some oft-repeated phrase, such as 'Absolutely first-rate!', Barkis is willin'!',[1] etc. This over-simplified view of people we find even in the great Molière. Harpagon is a miser and nothing else, although he might have been both miserly and a first-class financier, a loving father, a good citizen. And, what is worse, his 'defect' is in fact extremely advantageous to both his daughter and his son-in-law, who are his heirs and are thus the last people who ought to blame him if they have to wait a little before gathering the fruits of his parsimony. So I do not believe in 'theatrical characters'. And these summary judgements that authors pronounce upon people – 'He is stupid, he is brutal, he is

[1] Thus in the original; Strindberg knew his Dickens.

jealous, he is mean', etc. – ought to be challenged by naturalists, who know how richly complex a human soul is, and who are aware that 'vice' has a reverse image not dissimilar to virtue.

Since they are modern characters, living in an age of transition more urgently hysterical at any rate than the age which preceded it, I have drawn my people as split and vacillating, a mixture of the old and the new. And I think it not improbable that modern ideas may, through the media of newspapers and conversation, have seeped down into the social stratum which exists below stairs.

My souls (or characters) are agglomerations of past and present cultures, scraps from books and newspapers, fragments of humanity, torn shreds of once-fine clothing that has become rags, in just the way that a human soul is patched together. I have also provided a little documentation of character development, by making the weaker repeat words stolen from the stronger, and permitting the characters to borrow 'ideas', or, as the modern phrase is, accept suggestions from each other.

Miss Julie is a modern character – not that the half-woman, the man-hater, has not existed in every age, but because, now that she has been discovered, she has stepped forward into the limelight and begun to make a noise. The half-woman is a type that pushes herself to the front, nowadays selling herself for power, honours, decorations and diplomas, as formerly she used to for money. She is synonymous with corruption. They are a poor species, for they do not last, but unfortunately they propagate their like by the wretchedness they cause; and degenerate men seem unconsciously to choose their mates from among them, so that their number is increased. They engender an indeterminate sex to whom life is a torture, but fortunately they go under, either because they cannot adapt themselves to reality, or because their repressed instinct breaks out uncontrollably, or because their hopes of attaining equality with men are shattered. It is a tragic type, providing the spectacle of a desperate battle against Nature – and tragic also as a Romantic heritage now being dissipated by Naturalism, which thinks that the only good lies in happiness – and happiness is something that only a strong and hardy species can achieve.

But Miss Julie is also a relic of the old warrior nobility, which is now disappearing in favour of the new neurotic or intellectual nobility; a victim of the discord which a mother's 'crime' implanted in a family; a victim of the errors of her age, of circumstances, and of her own flawed constitution, all of which add up to the equivalent of the old concept of Destiny or the Universal Law. The naturalist has abolished guilt with God, but he cannot expunge the consequences of her action – punishment, and prison, or the fear of it – for the simple reason that, whether or not he acquits her, the consequences remain. One's injured fellow-beings are not as indulgent as outsiders who have not suffered can afford to be. Even if her father felt impelled to postpone the moment of Nemesis, vengeance would be taken on his daughter, as it is here, by that innate or acquired sense of honour which the upper classes inherit – from where? From barbarism, from their Aryan forefathers, from medieval chivalry. It is very beautiful, but nowadays it is fatal to the continuation of the species. It is the nobleman's *hara-kiri*, the Japanese law of inner conscience which commands a man to slit his stomach when another has insulted him, and which survives in a modified form in that ancient privilege of the nobility, the duel. Thus, the servant, Jean, lives; but Miss Julie cannot live without honour. The slave has this advantage over the knight, that he lacks the latter's fatal preoccupation with honour; but in all of us Aryans there is a little knight or Don Quixote who makes us sympathise with the man who kills himself because he has committed a dishonourable act and thereby lost his honour. We are aristocrats enough to be sad when we see the mighty fallen and stinking corpse-like on the garbage-heap – yes, even if the fallen should arise and make atonement by honourable action. The servant Jean is the type who founds a species; in him, we trace the process of differentiation. He was the son of a poor peasant, and has now educated himself to the point where he is a potential gentleman. He has proved a quick student, possesses finely developed senses (smell, taste, sight), and an eye for beauty. He has already risen in the world, and is strong enough not to worry about using other people's shoulders to climb on. He has already reacted against his fellow servants, whom he despises as representing the world which he has left behind him; he fears them and shrinks from them because they know his secrets, sniff

out his intentions, envy his rise and hopefully await his fall.
Hence his dual, uncrystallised character, wavering between
sympathy for the upper class and hatred of those who constitute
it. He is, as he himself says, an aristocrat; he has learned the
secrets of good society, is polished but coarse underneath; he
knows how to wear a tail-coat, but can offer us no guarantee that
his body is clean beneath it.

He respects Miss Julie, but is afraid of Christine, because she
knows his dangerous secrets; and he is sufficiently callous not to
allow the events of the night to interfere with his future plans.
With the brutality of a slave and the indifference of a tyrant he
can look at blood without fainting and shake off misfortune. So
he survives the battle unharmed, and will quite possibly end as
an *hôtelier*; and even if he does not become a Romanian count, his
son will probably get to university and very likely end up on the
bench.

Incidentally, the information he gives us about the lower
classes' view of life as seen from below is by no means negligible
– when, that is, he speaks the truth, which is not often, for his
tendency is to say what is likely to prove to his own advantage
rather than what is true. When Miss Julie throws out the
suggestion that the lower classes find the pressure from above
intolerable, Jean naturally agrees, because he wants to win her
sympathy, but he immediately corrects himself when he sees the
advantage of differentiating between himself and the mass.

Apart from the fact that Jean's star is rising, he has the whip-
hand of Miss Julie simply because he is a man. Sexually he is an
aristocrat by virtue of his masculine strength, his more finely
developed senses and his ability to seize the initiative. His sense
of inferiority arises chiefly from the social *milieu* in which he
temporarily finds himself, and he will probably throw it off when
he discards his livery.

His slave-mentality expresses itself in his respect for the Count
(the boots) and in his religious superstition; but he respects the
Count principally as the holder of the social position which he
himself covets. And this respect remains even when he has won
the daughter of the house and seen the emptiness of that pretty
shell.

I do not think that any 'love relationship' in the higher sense can exist between two spirits of such unequal quality, and I have therefore made Miss Julie imagine herself to be in love so as to excuse her action and escape her feeling of guilt; and I make Jean fancy that he might be able to fall in love with her, provided he could improve his social standing. I think it is the same with love as with the hyacinth, which has to strike roots in darkness before it can produce a strong flower. With these two, it shoots up, flowers and goes to seed in a moment, and that is why it so quickly dies.

What of Christine? She is a female slave, utterly conventional, bound to her stove and stuffed full of religion and morality, which serve her as both blinkers and scapegoats. She goes to church in order to be able to shift the guilt of her domestic pilferings on to Jesus, and get herself recharged with innocence. She is a supporting character, and I have therefore deliberately portrayed her as I did the priest and the doctor in *The Father;* I wanted them to appear everyday human beings, as provincial priests and doctors usually are. And if these supporting characters seem somewhat abstract, that is because ordinary people are, to a certain degree, abstract in the performance of their daily work – conventional, and showing only one side of themselves – and as long as the spectator feels no need to see their other sides, my abstract portrayal of them will serve well enough.

Finally, the dialogue. Here I have somewhat broken with tradition by not making my characters catechists who sit asking stupid questions in order to evoke some witty retort. I have avoided the symmetrical, mathematically constructed dialogue of the type favoured in France, and have allowed their minds to work irregularly, as people's do in real life, when, in conversation, no subject is fully exhausted, but one mind discovers in another a cog which it has a chance to engage. Consequently, the dialogue, too, wanders, providing itself in the opening scenes with matter which is later taken up, worked upon, repeated, expanded and added to, like the theme in a musical composition.

The plot is, I fancy, passable enough, and since it really only concerns two persons I have confined myself to them, introducing but one minor character, a cook, and making the unhappy spirit of the father hover over and behind the whole of the action. I have done this because I believe that what most interests people today is the psychological process. Our prying minds are not content merely with seeing something happen – they must know why it happens. We want to see the wires, see the machinery, examine the box with the false bottom, finger the magic ring to find the join, look at the cards to see how they are marked.

In this context I have been mindful of the realistic novels of the Goncourt brothers, which have attracted me more than anything else in contemporary literature.

On the question of technique, I have, by way of experiment, eliminated all intervals. I have done this because I believe that our declining capacity for illusion is possibly affected by intervals, which give the spectator time to reflect and thereby withdraw from the suggestive influence of the author-hypnotist. My play will probably run for about one and a half hours, and if people can listen to a lecture, a sermon or a parliamentary debate for that length of time, I think they should be able to endure a play for ninety minutes. As long ago as 1872, in one of my first dramatic attempts, *The Outlaw*, I aimed at this concentrated form, though with little success. I originally plotted it in five acts, and had already completed it before I noticed how broken and restless was its effect. I burned it, and from the ashes arose a single, long, integrated act of some fifty printed pages, which played for a full hour. This form is by no means new, though it appears at present to be my monopoly, and perhaps, thanks to the changing laws of taste, it may prove appropriate to the spirit of our time. My ultimate hope would be to educate an audience to the point where they will be able to sit through a full evening in the theatre without an interval, But one would have to examine the matter first. Meanwhile, in order to provide short periods of rest for the audience and the actors, without allowing the former to escape from my world of illusion, I have used three art-forms all of which properly belong to the drama – namely, the monologue, mime, and ballet. These were originally a part of ancient tragedy, the monody having developed into the monologue and the Greek chorus into ballet.

The monologue is nowadays abominated by our realists as

being contrary to reality, but if I motivate it I make it realistic, and can thus use it to advantage. It is after all realistic that a speaker should walk up and down alone in his room reading his speech aloud, that an actor should rehearse his part aloud, a servant-girl talk to her cat, a mother prattle to her child, an old maid jabber at her parrot, a sleeper talk in his sleep. And, to give the actor the chance for once to create for himself, and get off the author's leash, it is better that monologues should be implied rather than specified. For, since it matters little what one says in one's sleep, or to one's parrot or cat (for it does not influence the action), so a talented actor, attuned to the atmosphere and situation, may be able to improvise better than the author, who cannot calculate in advance how much needs to be said, or for how long the audience will accept the illusion.

As is known, the Italian theatre has, in certain instances, returned to improvisation and thereby created actors who themselves create, on the author's blueprint. This may well be a step forward, or even a new species of art, of which we shall be able to say that it is an art that engenders art.

Where a monologue would seem unrealistic, I have resorted to mime, which leaves the player even more freedom to create and so gain independent recognition. But in order not to make too great a demand upon the audience, I have allowed music, well motivated by the midsummer dance, to exercise its illusory power during the dumb play. Here I would ask the musical director to take care when choosing his pieces not to evoke an alien atmosphere by echoes from popular operettas or dance tunes, or folk melodies with specific associations.

The ballet which I have introduced must not be smudged into a so-called 'crowd scene', because crowd scenes are always badly acted, and a mob of buffoons would seize the chance to be clever and so destroy the illusion. Since simple people do not improvise when they wish to be spiteful, but use ready-to-hand material, I have not written new words for them but have borrowed a little-known song which I discovered myself in the countryside near Stockholm. The words are circumlocutory rather than direct, but that is as it should be, for the cunning (weakness) of servile people is not of the type that engages in direct assault. So there must be no chattering or clowning in what is, after all, a serious piece of

action, no coarse sniggering in a situation which drives the nails
into the coffin of a noble house.

As regards the décor, I have borrowed from the impressionist
painters asymmetry and suggestion (i.e., the part rather than the
whole), believing that I have thereby helped to further my
illusion. The fact that one does not see the whole room and all
the furniture leaves room for surmise – in other words, the
audience's imagination is set in motion and completes its own
picture. I have also profited by eliminating those tiresome exits
through doors; for stage doors are made of canvas and flap at the
slightest touch; they will not even allow an angry father to
express his fury by stumping out after a bad dinner and
slamming the door 'so that the whole house shakes'. (In the
theatre, the door simply waves.) I have likewise confined myself
to a single set, both to enable the characters to accustom
themselves to their *milieu*, and to get away from the tradition of
scenic luxury. But when one has only one set, one is entitled to
demand that it be realistic – though nothing is more difficult than
to make a room which looks like a room, however skilful the
artist may be at creating fire-spouting volcanoes and waterfalls.
Even if the walls have to be of canvas, it is surely time to stop
painting them with shelves and kitchen utensils. We have so
many other stage conventions in which we are expected to
believe that we may as well avoid overstraining our imagination
by asking it to believe in painted saucepans.

I have placed the rear wall and the table at an angle so that the
actors shall be able to face each other and be seen in demi-profile
when they sit opposite each other at the table. In a performance
of the opera *Aida* I once saw a backcloth at an angle which led
one's eyes off into an unknown perspective: nor did it look as
though it had been arranged thus simply out of a spirit of
reaction against the boredom of straight lines.

Another perhaps not unnecessary innovation would be the
removal of the footlights. This illumination from below is said to
serve the purpose of making actors fatter in the face; but I would
like to ask: 'Why should all actors be fat in the face?' Does not
this under-lighting annihilate all subtle expressions in the lower
half of the face, particularly around the mouth? Does it not falsify
the shape of the nose, and throw shadows up over the eyes? Even

if this were not so, one thing is certain: that pain is caused to the actors' eyes, so that any realistic expression is lost. For the footlights strike the retina on parts of it which are normally protected (except among sailors, who see the sun reflected from the water), so that one seldom sees any attempt at ocular expression other than fierce glares either to the side or up towards the gallery, when the whites of the eyes become visible. Perhaps this is also the cause of that tiresome habit, especially among actresses, of fluttering eyelashes. And when anyone on the stage wishes to speak with his eyes, he has no alternative but to look straight at the audience, thereby entering into direct contact with them outside the framework of the play – a bad habit which rightly or wrongly, is known as 'greeting one's friends'.

Would not side-lights of sufficient power (with reflectors, or some such device) endow the actor with this new resource, enabling him to reinforce his mime with his principal weapon of expression, the movement of his eyes?

I have few illusions of being able to persuade the actor to play *to* the audience and not with them, though this would be desirable. I do not dream that I shall ever see the full back of an actor throughout the whole of an important scene, but I do fervently wish that vital scenes should not be played opposite the prompter's box as though they were duets milking applause. I would have them played at whatever spot the situation might demand. So no revolutions, but simply small modifications; for to turn the stage into a room with the fourth wall missing, so that some of the furniture would have its back to the audience, would, I suppose, at this juncture, simply serve as a distraction.

A word about make-up; which I dare not hope will be listened to by the ladies, who prefer beauty to truth. But the actor might well ponder whether it is to his advantage to paint an abstract character upon his face which will remain sitting there like a mask. Imagine a gentleman dipping his finger into soot and drawing a line of bad temper between his eyes, and suppose that, wearing this permanently fierce expression, he were called upon to deliver a line smiling? How dreadful would be the result! And how is this false forehead, smooth as a billiard ball, to wrinkle when the old man gets really angry?

In a modern psychological drama, where the subtler reactions should be mirrored in the face rather than in gesture and sound, it would surely be best to experiment with strong side-lights on a small stage and with the actor wearing no make-up, or at best a minimum.

If we could then dispense with the visible orchestra, with their distracting lampshades and faces turned towards the audience; if we could have the stalls raised so that the spectator's sightline would be above the actors' knees; if we could get rid of the side-boxes (my particular *bête noire*), with their tittering diners and ladies nibbling at cold collations, and have complete darkness in the auditorium during the performance, and, first and foremost, a *small* stage and a *small* auditorium – then perhaps a new drama might emerge, and the theatre might once again become a place for educated people. While we await such a theatre, one must write to create a stock of plays in readiness for the repertoire that will, some day, be needed.

I have made an attempt! If it has failed, there will, I hope, be time enough to make another!

Miss Julie

This translation of *Miss Julie* was presented by the National Theatre at the Chichester Festival on 27 July 1965, and subsequently at the Old Vic Theatre, London, on 8 March 1966, both times with the following cast:

Miss Julie   Maggie Smith
Jean, *her father's valet*   Albert Finney
Christine, *her father's cook* Jeanne Watts
Other servants   Chloe Ashcroft, Elizabeth Burger, Kay Gallic, Jennie Heslewood, Caroline John, Carolyn Jones, Pauline Taylor, Michael Byrne, Alan Collins, Neil Fitzpatrick, John Hallam, Ron Pember, Edward Petherbridge, Ronald Pickup, David Ryall, John Savident

Musicians   Sydney Bliss, Pierre Tas, Henry Krein
Designed by Richard Negri
Directed by Michael Elliott

On 27 October 1971 it was performed by the Royal Shakespeare Company at The Place, Euston Road. The cast was:

Miss Julie   Helen Mirren
Jean   Donal McCann
Christine   Heather Canning
Other servants   Mary Allen, Isla Blair, Colin Edwynn, Michael Egan, Ron Forfar, Julian Glover, Patrick Godfrey, Edward Phillips, Holly Wilson

Designed by Daphne Dare
Directed by Robin Phillips

This production was subsequently filmed, with the same cast and director.

The action takes place in the Count's kitchen on Midsummer Night.

A large kitchen, the roof and side walls of which are concealed by drapes and borders. The rear wall rises at an angle from the left; on it, to the left, are two shelves with utensils of copper, iron and pewter. The shelves are lined with scalloped paper. Over to the right we can see three-quarters of a big, arched exit porch, with twin glass doors, through which can be seen a fountain with a statue of Cupid, lilac bushes in bloom, and tall Lombardy poplars. On the left of the stage is visible the corner of a big tiled stove, with a section of an overhead hood to draw away fumes. To the right, one end of the kitchen table, of white pine, with some chairs. The stove is decorated with birch-leaves; the floor is strewn with juniper twigs. On the end of the table is a big Japanese spice-jar containing flowering lilacs. An ice-box, a scullery table, a sink. Above the door is a big old-fashioned bell, of the alarm type. To the left of this emerges a speaking-tube.

Christine *is standing at the stove, frying in a pan. She is dressed in a light cotton dress, with apron.* **Jean** *enters, dressed in livery and carrying a pair of big riding boots, with spurs. He puts them down on the floor where we can see them.*

Jean   Miss Julie's gone mad again tonight, completely mad!

Christine   Oh, you're here at last?

Jean   I went with his lordship to the station, and on the way back I just popped into the barn to watch the dancing, and who do I see but Miss Julie leading the dance with the gamekeeper? But as soon as she sees me, she rushes across and offers her arm for the ladies' waltz. And then she danced like – I've never known the like! She's mad.

Christine   She always has been. Especially this last fortnight, since the engagement got broken off.

Jean   Yes, what about that? He was a gentleman, even if he wasn't rich. Ach, they don't know their own minds. (*He sits down at the end of the table.*) It's odd, though, that a young lady should choose to stay at home with the servants, on Midsummer Eve, eh? rather than go off to her relations with her father.

Christine   Oh, I expect she doesn't feel like seeing anyone after that hullaballoo she had with her young man.

Jean   Very likely! He knew how to stand up for himself, though. Know how it happened, Christine? I saw it, you know, though I took care not to let on I had.

Christine   No! You saw it?

Jean   Indeed I did. They were down at the stable yard one evening, and Miss Julie was putting him through his paces, as she called it – do you know what that meant? She made him leap over her riding whip, the way you teach a dog to jump. He leaped twice, and each time she gave him a cut; but the third time, he snatched the whip out of her hand and broke it across his knee. And that was the last we saw of him.

Christine   Was that what happened? You can't mean it.

Jean   Yes, that's the way it was. Now, what have you got to tempt me with this evening, Christine?

Christine (*serves from the pan and lays a place*)   Oh, just a bit of kidney I cut from the joint.

Jean (*smells the food*)   Lovely! *Ceci est mon grand délice!* (*He feels the plate.*) You might have warmed the plate, though.

Christine   You're fussier than his lordship himself, once you start. (*She pulls his hair affectionately.*)

Jean (*angrily*)   Don't pull my hair. You know how sensitive I am.

Christine   Now, now. It's only love.

Jean *eats.* **Christine** *brings a bottle of beer.*

Jean   Beer – on Midsummer Eve? No, thank you. I can do better than that. (*He opens a drawer in the table and takes out a bottle of red wine with yellow sealing-wax on the cork.*) See that? Yellow seal! Give me a glass, now. A wine glass, I'm drinking this *pur.*

Christine (*goes back to the stove and puts a small saucepan on*)   God have mercy on whoever gets you for a husband. I never met such a fusspot.

Jean   Oh, rubbish. You'd be jolly pleased to get a gentleman like me. And I don't think you've lost anything through people calling you my fiancée. (*He tastes the wine.*) Good! Very good! Just not quite sufficiently *chambré*. (*He warms the glass with his hand.*) We bought this one in Dijon. Four francs a litre it cost – and then there was the bottling – and the duty. What are you cooking now? The smell's infernal.

Christine Oh, some filthy muck Miss Julie wants for Diana.

Jean Please express yourself more delicately, Christine. But why should you have to cook for that confounded dog on Midsummer Eve? Is it ill?

Christine It's ill all right! It managed to slip out with the gatekeeper's pug, and now it's in trouble – and *that* Miss Julie won't allow.

Jean Miss Julie is stuck-up about some things, in others she demeans herself, exactly like her ladyship when she was alive. She was most at home in the kitchen or the stables, but one horse wasn't enough to pull her carriage. She went around with dirty cuffs, but there had to be a crest on every button. Miss Julie, now, to return to her – she doesn't bother about herself and her person. To my mind, she is not what one would call a lady. Just now, when she was dancing in the barn, she grabbed the gamekeeper from Anna and made him dance with her. We'd never do that – but that's how it is when the gentry try to act common – they become really common. But she's a magnificent creature! What a figure! Ah! What shoulders! and – et cetera!

Christine No need to overdo it. I've heard what Clara says, and she dresses her.

Jean Oh, Clara! You women are always jealous of each other. I've been out riding with her – and the way she dances –!

Christine Well, aren't you going to dance with me, when I'm ready?

Jean Yes, of course.

Christine Promise?

Jean Promise? When I say I'll do a thing, I do it. Thank you for that, it was very nice. (*He corks the bottle.*)

Miss Julie (*in the doorway, talking to someone outside*)   I'll be back immediately. Don't wait for me.

Jean *hides the bottle in the drawer of the table and gets up respectfully.*

Miss Julie (*enters and goes up to* **Christine** *by the stove*)   Well, is it ready?

Christine *indicates that* **Jean** *is present.*

Jean (*gallantly*)   Have you ladies secrets to discuss?

Miss Julie (*flips him in the face with her handkerchief*)   Don't be inquisitive!

Jean   Ah! Charming, that smell of violets.

Miss Julie (*coquettishly*)   Impertinent! So you know about perfumes, too? You certainly know how to dance – stop looking, now, go away!

Jean (*boldly, yet respectfully*)   Is this some magic brew you ladies are preparing on Midsummer Eve, which will reveal the future and show whom fate has in store for you?

Miss Julie (*sharply*)   You'd need sharp eyes to see him. (*To* **Christine**.) Pour it into a bottle, and cork it well. Come now, and dance a schottische with me, Jean.

Jean (*slowly*)   I don't wish to seem disrespectful, but this dance I had promised to Christine –

Miss Julie   Well, she can have another dance with you, can't you, Christine? Won't you lend me Jean?

Christine   That's hardly up to me. If Miss Julie condescends, it's not his place to refuse. Go ahead, Jean, and thank madam for the honour.

Jean   To be frank, without wishing to offend, I wonder if it would be wise for Miss Julie to dance twice in succession with the same partner. These people soon start talking –

Miss Julie (*flares up*)   Talking? What kind of talk? What do you mean?

Jean (*politely*) If madam doesn't understand, I must speak more plainly. It looks bad if you show a preference for one of your servants while others are waiting to be similarly honoured –

Miss Julie Preference! What an idea! I am astounded. I, the lady of the house, honour my servants by attending their dance, and when I take the floor I want to dance with someone who knows how to lead. I don't want to be made ridiculous –

Jean As madam commands. I am at your service.

Miss Julie (*softly*) Don't regard it as a command. Tonight we are ordinary people trying to be happy, and all rank is laid aside. Come, give me your arm! Don't worry, Christine! I won't steal your lover!

Jean *offers* **Miss Julie** *his arm, and escorts her out.*

Pantomime

This should be played as though the actress were actually alone. When the occasion calls for it she should turn her back on the audience. She does not look towards them; and must not hasten her movements as though afraid lest they should grow impatient.

Christine *alone. A violin can be faintly heard in the distance, playing a schottische.* **Christine** *hums in time with the music; clears up after* **Jean***, washes the plate at the sink, dries it and puts it away in a cupboard. Then she removes her apron, takes a small mirror from a drawer, props it against the pot of lilac on the table; lights a candle and warms a curling-iron, with which she then crisps the hair over her forehead. Goes out into the doorway and listens. Returns to the table. Finds* **Miss Julie***'s handkerchief, which the latter has forgotten; picks it up and smells it; then, spreads it out, as though thinking of something else, stretches it, smooths it, folds it into quarters, etc.*

Jean (*enters alone*) No, she really *is* mad! What a way to dance! Everyone was grinning at her from behind the doors. What do you make of it, Christine?

Christine   Oh, she's got her monthly coming on, and then she always acts strange. Well, are you going to dance with me now?

Jean   You're not angry with me for leaving you like that – ?

Christine   No, a little thing like that doesn't bother me. Besides, I know my place –

Jean (*puts his arm round her waist*)   You're a sensible girl, Christine. You'd make a good wife –

Miss Julie (*enters; is disagreeably surprised; speaks with forced lightness*) Well, you're a fine gentleman, running away from your partner like that!

Jean   On the contrary, Miss Julie. As you see, I have hastened to return to the partner I forsook!

Miss Julie (*changes her tone*)   Do you know, you dance magnificently. But why are you wearing uniform on Midsummer Eve? Take it off at once.

Jean   Then I must ask your ladyship to step outside for a moment. I have my black coat here – (*Gestures right.*)

Miss Julie   Does my presence embarrass you? Can't you change a coat with me here? You'd better go into your room, then. Or stay, and I'll turn my back.

Jean   With your ladyship's permission.

He goes right. We see his arm as he changes his coat.

Miss Julie (*to* **Christine**)   Christine, Jean is very familiar with you. Are you engaged to him?

Christine   Engaged? If you like. We call it that.

Miss Julie   Call – ?

Christine   Well, you've been engaged yourself, madam –

Miss Julie   We were properly engaged.

Christine   Didn't come to anything, though, did it?

Jean *enters in black tails and a black bowler hat.*

Miss Julie   *Très gentil, monsieur Jean! Très gentil!*

Jean   *Vous voulez plaisanter, madame!*

Miss Julie   *Et vous voulez parler français!* Where did you learn that?

Jean   In Switzerland. I was wine waiter at the biggest hotel in Lucerne.

Miss Julie   You look quite the gentleman in those tails. *Charmant!* (*She sits at the table.*)

Jean   Oh, you're flattering me.

Miss Julie (*haughtily*)   Flattering *you*?

Jean   My natural modesty forbids me to suppose that you would pay a truthful compliment to one so humble as myself, so I assumed you were exaggerating, for which I believe the polite word is flattering.

Miss Julie   Where did you learn to talk like that? You must have spent a lot of your time at the theatre.

Jean   Yes. And I've been around a bit, too.

Miss Julie   But you were born here, weren't you?

Jean   My father worked on the next farm to yours. I used to see you when I was a child, though you wouldn't remember me.

Miss Julie   No, really?

Jean   Yes. I remember one time especially – no, I oughtn't to mention that.

Miss Julie   Oh yes! Tell me. Come on! Just this once.

Jean   No, I really couldn't now. Some other time, perhaps.

Miss Julie   Some other time means never. Is it so dangerous to tell it now?

Jean   It isn't dangerous, but I'd rather not. Look at her! (*He indicates* **Christine**, *who has fallen asleep in a chair by the stove.*)

Miss Julie   A charming wife she'll make. Does she snore too?

Jean   She doesn't do that, but she talks in her sleep.

Miss Julie (*cynically*)   How do you know?

Jean (*coolly*)   I've heard her.

Pause. They look at each other.

Miss Julie   Why don't you sit?

Jean   I wouldn't permit myself to do that in your presence.

Miss Julie   But if I order you to?

Jean   Then I shall obey.

Miss Julie   Sit, then. No, wait. Can you give me something to drink first?

Jean   I don't know what we have in the ice-cabinet. Only beer, I think.

Miss Julie   What do you mean, only beer? My taste is very simple. I prefer it to wine.

Jean *takes a bottle of beer from the ice-cabinet; opens it, gets a glass and plate from the cupboard and serves her.*

Jean   Mademoiselle!

Miss Julie   Thank you. Won't you have something yourself?

Jean   I'm not much of a beer drinker, but if madam orders me –

Miss Julie   Orders? Surely you know that a gentleman should never allow a lady to drink alone.

Jean   That's perfectly true. (*He opens another bottle and pours a glass.*)

Miss Julie   Drink my health, now! (**Jean** *hesitates.*) Are you shy?

Jean (*kneels in a parody of a romantic attitude, and raises his glass*)   To my mistress's health!

Miss Julie   Bravo! Now kiss my shoe, and the ceremony is complete.

Jean *hesitates, then boldly takes her foot in his hands and kisses it lightly.*

Miss Julie   Excellent. You ought to have been an actor.

Jean (*gets up*)   We mustn't go on like this, Miss Julie. Someone might come in and see us.

Miss Julie   What then?

Jean   People would talk, that's all. And if you knew how their tongues were wagging up there just now –

Miss Julie   What kind of thing were they saying? Tell me. Sit down.

Jean (*sits*)   I don't want to hurt you, but they were using expressions which – which hinted that – well, you can guess! You aren't a child, and when people see a lady drinking alone with a man – let alone a servant – on Midsummer Eve – then –

Miss Julie   Then what? Anyway, we're not alone. Christine is here.

Jean   Asleep.

Miss Julie   Then I shall wake her. (*She gets up.*) Christine! Christine! Are you asleep?

Christine *mumbles to herself in her sleep.*

Miss Julie   Christine! My God, she is asleep!

Christine (*in her sleep*)   Are his lordship's boots brushed? Put on the coffee. Quickly, quickly, quickly! (*She laughs, then grunts.*)

Miss Julie (*takes her by the nose*)   Will you wake up?

Jean (*sharply*)   Leave her alone!

Miss Julie (*haughtily*)   What!

Jean   People who stand at a stove all day get tired when night comes. And sleep is something to be respected –

Miss Julie (*changes tack*)   A gallant thought, and one that does you honour. (*She holds out her hand to* **Jean**.) Come outside then, and pick some lilac for me.

During the following dialogue, **Christine** *wakes and wanders drowsily right to go to bed.*

Jean   With you?

Miss Julie   With me.

Jean   Impossible. I couldn't.

Miss Julie   I don't understand. Surely you don't imagine – ?

Jean   I don't, but other people might.

Miss Julie   What? That I should have an *amour* with a servant?

Jean   I'm not being conceited, but such things have happened – and to these people, nothing is sacred.

Miss Julie   Quite the little aristocrat, aren't you?

Jean   Yes, I am.

Miss Julie   If I choose to step down –

Jean   Don't step down, Miss Julie, take my advice. No one will believe you did it freely. People will always say you fell –

Miss Julie   I have a higher opinion of people than you. Come and see! Come.

She fixes him with her eyes.

Jean   You know, you're strange.

Miss Julie   Perhaps. But so are you. Everything is strange. Life, people, everything, is a scum which drifts, drifts on and on across the water until it sinks, sinks. I have a dream which recurs from time to time, and I'm reminded of it now. I've climbed to the top of a pillar, and am sitting there, and I can see no way to descend. When I look down, I become dizzy, but I must come down – but I haven't the courage to jump. I can't stay up there, and I long to fall, but I don't fall. And yet I know I shall find no peace till I come down, no rest till I come down, down to the ground. And if I could get down, I should want to burrow my way deep into the earth . . . Have you ever felt anything like that?

Jean   No. I dream that I'm lying under a high tree in a dark wood. I want to climb, up, up to the top, and look round over the bright landscape where the sun is shining – plunder the bird's nest up there where the gold eggs lie. And I climb and climb, but the trunk is so thick and slippery, and it's so far to the first branch. But I know that if I could only get to that first branch, I'd climb my way to the top as though up a ladder. I haven't reached it yet, but I shall reach it, even if it's only in a dream.

Miss Julie   Why do we stand here talking about dreams? Come, now! Just into the park!

She offers him her arm, and they go.

Jean   We must sleep with nine midsummer flowers under our pillows tonight, Miss Julie, and our dreams will come true!

They turn in the doorway. **Jean** *puts a hand to one of his eyes.*

Miss Julie   Have you something in your eye?

Jean   It's nothing. Only a speck of dust. It'll be all right soon.

Miss Julie   My sleeve must have brushed it. Sit down and I'll take it out. (*She takes him by the arm, makes him sit, takes his head and pushes it backwards, and tries to remove the dust with the corner of her handkerchief.*) Sit still now, quite still! (*She slaps his hands.*) Come, obey me! I believe you're trembling, you great, strong lout! (*She feels his bicep.*) What muscles you have!

Jean (*warningly*)   Miss Julie!

Miss Julie   Yes, monsieur Jean?

Jean   *Attention! Je ne suis qu'un homme!*

Miss Julie   Sit still, will you! There! Now it's gone. Kiss my hand and thank me.

Jean (*gets up*)   Miss Julie, listen to me. Christine's gone to bed now – will you listen to me!

Miss Julie   Kiss my hand first.

Jean Listen to me!

Miss Julie Kiss my hand first.

Jean All right. But you've only yourself to blame.

Miss Julie For what?

Jean For what? Are you a child? You're twenty-five. Don't you know it's dangerous to play with fire?

Miss Julie Not for me. I am insured.

Jean (*boldly*) No, you're not. And if you are, there's inflammable material around that isn't.

Miss Julie Meaning you?

Jean Yes. Not because I'm me, but because I'm a young man –

Miss Julie Of handsome appearance! What incredible conceit! A Don Juan, perhaps? Or a Joseph! Yes, upon my word, I do believe you're a Joseph!

Jean Do you?

Miss Julie I almost fear it.

Jean *moves boldly forward and tries to take her round the waist to kiss her.*

Miss Julie (*slaps him*) Stop it!

Jean Are you joking or serious?

Miss Julie Serious.

Jean Then you were being serious just now too. You play games too seriously, and that's dangerous. Well, now I'm tired of this game and with your permission I'll get back to my work. His lordship's boots must be ready in time, and it's long past midnight.

Miss Julie Forget the boots.

Jean No. They're part of my job, which doesn't include being your playmate. And never will. I flatter myself I'm above that.

Miss Julie   Aren't we proud!

Jean   In some respects. In others, not.

Miss Julie   Have you ever been in love?

Jean   We don't use that word. But I've been fond of a lot of girls, and once I was sick because I couldn't get the one I wanted. Yes, sick, do you hear, like those princes in the *Arabian Nights*, who couldn't eat or sleep because of love.

Miss Julie   Who was she? (**Jean** *is silent.*) Who was she?

Jean   You cannot order me to answer that.

Miss Julie   If I ask you as an equal? As a friend! Who was she?

Jean   You.

Miss Julie (*sits*)   How absurd!

Jean   Yes, if you like. It was absurd. Look, this was the story I didn't want to tell you just now – but now I will tell you. Do you know how the world looks from down there? No, you don't. Like hawks and eagles, whose backs one seldom sees because most of the time they hover above you! I lived in a hut with seven brothers and sisters and a pig, out in the grey fields where never a tree grew. But from the window I could see the wall of his lordship's park, with apple trees rising above it. It was the Garden of Paradise, and there stood many evil angels with flaming swords to guard it. But despite them I and other boys found a way in to the tree of life – You despise me now?

Miss Julie   Oh, I suppose all boys steal apples.

Jean   You can say that now, but you do despise me. However. One day I entered the garden with my mother, to weed the onion beds. On one side of the garden stood a Turkish pavilion in the shadow of jasmine trees and overgrown with honeysuckle. I'd never seen such a building. I wondered what it could be for. People went in and came out again; and, one day, the door was left open. I crept in and saw the walls hung with pictures of kings and emperors, and there were red velvet curtains on the windows with tassels – ah, now you understand! It was the lavatory. I – (*He* *breaks a flower from the lilac and holds it beneath* **Miss Julie***'s nose.*) I'd never been inside the palace, never seen anything except the church – but this was more beautiful – and however my thoughts might stray, they always returned there. And gradually I began to long just once to experience the full ecstasy of actually – *enfin,* I tip-toed inside, saw and marvelled. But then – someone's coming! There was only one exit – for the lords and ladies. But for me – there was another – and I had no choice but to take it. (**Miss Julie**, *who has taken the lilac blossom, lets it fall on the table.*) Then I ran, broke through a raspberry hedge, charged across a strawberry patch, and found myself on a terrace with a rose garden. There I saw a pink dress and a pair of white stockings. You. I hid under a pile of weeds – *under,* can you imagine that? under thistles that pricked me and wet earth that stank like me. And I looked at you as you walked among the roses, and I thought: 'If it is true that a thief can enter heaven and dwell with the angels, then it's strange that a peasant's child here on earth cannot enter the great park and play with the Count's daughter.'

Miss Julie (*romantically*)   Do you suppose all poor children have had the same ideas as you?

Jean (*at first hesitant, then with conviction*)   Have *all* poor – ? Yes! Of course! Of course!

Miss Julie   It must be a terrible misfortune to be poor.

Jean (*deeply cut, speaks with strong emotion*)   Oh, Miss Julie! Oh! A dog may lie on the Countess's sofa, a horse may have its nose patted by a young lady's hand, but a servant – ! (*He changes his tone.*) Oh, now and then a man has strength enough to hoist himself up in the world, but how often does it happen? But do you know what I did? I ran down into the millstream with my clothes on. They dragged me out and beat me. But the following Sunday, when my father and all the others had gone to visit my grandmother, I managed to fix things so that I stayed at home. And then I scrubbed myself with soap and hot water, put on my best clothes, and went to church, in order that I might see you. I saw you, and returned home, determined to die. But I wanted to die beautifully, and pleasantly, without pain. Then I remembered it was dangerous to sleep under an elder bush. We

had a big one, in flower. I stripped it of everything it held, and
then I lay down in the oat-bin. Have you ever noticed how
beautiful oats are? Soft to the touch like human skin. Well, I shut
the lid and closed my eyes. I fell asleep, and woke up feeling
really very ill. But I didn't die, as you can see. What did I want? I
don't know. I had no hope of winning you, of course – but you
were a symbol to me of the hopelessness of my ever climbing out
of the class in which I was born.

Miss Julie   Do you know you're quite a *raconteur*? Did you ever
go to school?

Jean   A bit. But I've read a lot of novels, and gone to theatres.
And I've heard gentry talk. That's where I've learned most.

Miss Julie   Do you listen to what we say?

Jean   Certainly! And I've heard plenty, too, sitting on the
coachman's box or rowing the boat. One time I heard you and a
lady friend –

Miss Julie   Indeed? What did you hear?

Jean   Oh, I wouldn't care to repeat it. But it surprised me a
little. I couldn't imagine where you'd learned all those words.
Maybe at bottom there isn't as big a difference as people suppose
between people and – people.

Miss Julie   Oh, nonsense. We don't act like you do when
we're engaged.

Jean (*looks at her*)   Are you sure? Come, Miss Julie, you don't
have to play the innocent with me –

Miss Julie   The man to whom I offered my love was a
bastard.

Jean   That's what they always say – afterwards.

Miss Julie   Always?

Jean   I've heard the expression several times before on similar
occasions.

Miss Julie   What occasions?

Jean   Like the one in question. The last time I actually slept with a woman –

Miss Julie (*rises*)   Be quiet! I don't wish to hear any more.

Jean   *She* didn't want to, either. Strange. Well, have I your permission to go to bed?

Miss Julie (*softly*)   Go to bed? On Midsummer Eve?

Jean   Yes. Dancing with that pack up there doesn't greatly amuse me.

Miss Julie   Get the key of the boat and row me out on the lake, I want to see the sun rise.

Jean   Is that wise?

Miss Julie   You speak as though you were frightened of your reputation.

Jean   Why not? I don't want to make myself a laughing-stock and maybe get sacked without a reference, now that I'm beginning to make my way. And I think I have a certain responsibility towards Christine.

Miss Julie   Oh, I see, it's Christine now –

Jean   Yes, but you too. Take my advice. Go back to your room and go to bed.

Miss Julie   Am *I* to obey *you*?

Jean   For once. For your own sake, I beg you! It's late, drowsiness makes one drunk, one's head grows dizzy. Go to bed. Besides – if my ears don't deceive me – the other servants are coming here to look for me. And if they find us together, you are lost!

Approaching voices are heard, singing.

Voices
One young girl in a big dark wood!
Tridiridi-ralla, tridiridi-ra!
Met a boy she never should!
Tridiridi-ralla-ra!

Oh, lay me on the grass so soft!
Tridiridi-ralla, tridiridi-ra!
So her mm-mm-mm she lost!
Tridiridi-ralla-ra!

Oh, thank you dear, but I must go!
Tridiridi-ralla, tridiridi-ra!
Another loves me now . . . oh!
Tridiridi-ralla-ra!

Miss Julie   I know these people, and I love them, as I know they love me. Let them come here, and I'll prove it to you.

Jean   No, Miss Julie, they don't love you. They take your food, but once you've turned your back they spit at you. Believe me! Listen to them, listen to what they're singing! No, don't listen!

Miss Julie (*listens*)   What are they singing?

Jean   It's a filthy song. About you and me.

Miss Julie   How dare they! The traitors – !

Jean   Yes, but that's what they're like. One can't fight them. One can only run away.

Miss Julie   Run away? But where? We can't go out – or into Christine's room!

Jean   No. Into my room, then. We can't bother about conventions now. And you can trust me. I am your true, loyal and respectful – friend.

Miss Julie   But suppose – suppose they look for you in there?

Jean   I'll bolt the door. And if anyone tries to break in, I'll shoot. Come! (*He drops to his knees.*) Please! Come!

Miss Julie (*urgently*)   You promise –

Jean   I swear.

Miss Julie *runs out right,* **Jean** *hastens after her.*

Ballet

The peasants stream in, wearing their best clothes, with flowers in their hats and a fiddler at their head. A barrel of beer and a keg of schnapps decorated with greenery are set on the table, glasses are produced, and they drink. They form a ring and dance and mime, singing: 'One young girl in a big dark wood!' When this is finished, they go out singing.

Miss Julie *enters, alone. She sees the chaos in the kitchen, clasps her hands, then takes out a powder puff and powders her face.*

Jean (*enters, agitated*)   There – you see! And you heard. Do you think you can possibly stay here now?

Miss Julie   No. I don't. But what can we do?

Jean   Go away – travel – far away from here –

Miss Julie   Travel? Yes, but where?

Jean   To Switzerland, to the Italian lakes! Have you never been there?

Miss Julie   No. Is it beautiful there?

Jean   Ah! An eternal summer! Oranges, laurel trees – ah!

Miss Julie   But what shall we do there?

Jean   I'll start a hotel. *De luxe* – for *de luxe* people.

Miss Julie   Hotel?

Jean   Ah, that's a life, believe me! New faces all the time, new languages! Never a minute for worry or nerves, or wondering what to do. There's work to be done every minute, bells ringing night and day, trains whistling, carriages coming and going, and all the time the golden sovereigns roll into the till. Yes, that's the life!

Miss Julie   It sounds exciting. But – I – ?

Jean   Shall be the mistress of the house; the pearl of the establishment. With your looks – and your style – why, we're made! It'll be terrific! You'll sit at your desk like a queen, setting your slaves in motion by pressing an electric bell. The guests will

file before your throne, humbly laying their tribute upon your
table – you've no idea how people tremble when they get a bill in
their hand. I shall salt the bills, and you shall sugar them with
your prettiest smile! Oh, let's get away from here! (*He takes a
timetable from his pocket.*) Now, at once, by the next train! We'll be
in Malmö by 6.30, Hamburg 8.40 tomorrow morning, Frankfurt
to Basel will take a day, through the Gothard Pass – we'll be in
Como in, let me see, three days. Three days!

Miss Julie   It sounds wonderful. But, Jean – you must give me
courage. Tell me you love me. Come and kiss me.

Jean (*hesitates*)   I'd like to – but I daren't. Not in this house – not
again. Of course I love you – can you doubt it, Miss Julie?

Miss Julie (*shy, feminine*)   *Miss!* Call me Julie! There are no
barriers between us now. Call me Julie!

Jean (*tormented*)   I can't! There are still barriers between us – there
always will be, as long as we're in this house. There's the past,
there's his lordship – I've never met anyone I respected as I do him
– I only have to see his gloves on a chair and I feel like a small boy
– I only have to hear that bell ring and I jump like a frightened
horse – and when I see his boots standing there, so straight and
proud, I cringe. (*He kicks the boots.*) Superstition – ideas shoved into
our heads when we're children – but we can escape them. Come
to another country, a republic, and others will cringe before my
porter's livery – yes, they'll cringe, I tell you, but I shan't! I wasn't
born to cringe – I'm a man, I've got character, just let me get my
fingers on that first branch and watch me climb! Today I'm a
servant, but next year I'll own my own hotel, in ten years I'll be a
landed gentleman! Then I'll go to Romania, get a decoration –
why, I might – might, mind you – end up with a title.

Miss Julie   How wonderful!

Jean   Oh, in Romania I could buy myself a title. I'd be a count,
and you'd be a countess. My countess!

Miss Julie   What do I care about all that? That's what I'm
giving up now. Tell me you love me, otherwise – yes, otherwise –
what am I?

Jean   I'll tell you a thousand times – later. Only – not here. Above all, no emotional scenes, or it'll be all up with us. We must think this over coolly, like sensible people. (*He takes a cigar, cuts and lights it.*) Sit down there now, and I'll sit here and we'll talk as though nothing had happened.

Miss Julie (*desperately*)   Oh, my God! Have you no feelings?

Jean   I? No one has more feelings than I. But I can control them.

Miss Julie   A moment ago you could kiss my shoe – and now – !

Jean (*harshly*)   That was a moment ago. Now we've something else to think about.

Miss Julie   Don't speak so harshly to me.

Jean   I'm not speaking harshly. I'm talking sense. One folly has been committed, don't let's commit any more. His lordship may be here any moment, and by then we've got to decide what we're going to do with our lives. What do you think of my plans for our future? Do you approve of them?

Miss Julie   They seem to me quite sensible but – just one question. A big project like that needs a lot of capital. Have you that?

Jean (*chews his cigar*)   I? Certainly. I have my professional expertise, my experience, my knowledge of languages. We've adequate capital, I should say.

Miss Julie   But all that doesn't add up to the price of a railway ticket.

Jean   That's perfectly true; which is why I need a backer to advance me the money.

Miss Julie   Where are you going to find one quickly?

Jean   You'll find one, if you come with me.

Miss Julie   I couldn't. And I haven't any money of my own.

Pause.

Jean   Then our whole plan collapses.

Miss Julie   And – ?

Jean   Things must stay as they are.

Miss Julie   Do you suppose I'm going to remain under this roof as your whore? With *them* sniggering at me behind their fingers? Do you think I can look my father in the face after this? No! Take me away from here, from the shame and the dishonour – oh, what have I done, my God, my God! (*Sobs.*)

Jean   Come, don't start that. What have you done? The same as many others before you.

Miss Julie (*screams convulsively*)   Oh, now you despise me! I'm falling – I'm falling – !

Jean   Fall down to me, and I'll lift you up again.

Miss Julie   What dreadful power drew me to you? The attraction of the weak to the strong? Of the faller to the climber? Or was it love? Was this love? Do you know what love is?

Jean   I? Yes, of course. Do you think I've never had a woman before?

Miss Julie   How can you think and talk like that?

Jean   That's life as I've learned it, And that's me. Now calm down and stop acting the lady. We're both in the same boat now. Come here, my girl, and I'll give you a glass of wine. (*He opens the drawer, takes out the bottle of wine and fills two used glasses.*)

Miss Julie   Where did you get that wine from?

Jean   The cellar.

Miss Julie   My father's burgundy!

Jean   Is it too good for his son-in-law?

Miss Julie   And I drink beer! I!

Jean   That only proves you have an inferior palate to mine.

Miss Julie   Thief!

Jean   Going to tell?

Miss Julie   Oh, oh! Accomplice to a sneakthief! Was I drunk, was I dreaming? Midsummer Night! The night of innocent happiness –

Jean   Innocent? Hm!

Miss Julie (*paces to and fro*)   Is there anyone on this earth as miserable as I?

Jean   Why should you be miserable after such a conquest? Think of Christine in there. Don't you suppose she has feelings too?

Miss Julie   I thought so just now, but I don't any longer. Servants are servants –

Jean   And whores are whores.

Miss Julie (*kneels and clasps her hands*)   Oh, God in Heaven, end my miserable life! Save me from this mire into which I'm sinking! Save me, save me!

Jean   I can't deny I feel sorry for you. When I lay in the onion bed and saw you in the rose garden – I might as well tell you now – I had the same dirty thoughts as any small boy.

Miss Julie   You – who wanted to die for me?

Jean   The oat-bin? Oh, that was just talk.

Miss Julie   A lie?

Jean (*begins to get sleepy*)   More or less. I once read a story in a paper about a sweep who curled up in a wood-chest with some lilacs because he'd had a paternity order brought against him –

Miss Julie   I see. You're the kind who –

Jean   Well, I had to think up something. Women always fall for pretty stories.

Miss Julie   Swine!

Jean   *Merde!*

Miss Julie   And now you've managed to see the eagle's back –

Jean   Not exactly its back.

Miss Julie   And I was to be the first branch –

Jean   But the branch was rotten –

Miss Julie   I was to be the signboard of the hotel –

Jean   And I the hotel –

Miss Julie   I was to sit at your desk, attract your customers, fiddle your bills –

Jean   No, I'd have done that –

Miss Julie   Can a human soul become so foul?

Jean   Wash it, then!

Miss Julie   Servant, lackey, stand up when I speak!

Jean   Servant's whore, lackey's bitch, shut your mouth and get out of here. You dare to stand there and call me foul? Not one of my class ever behaved the way you've done tonight. Do you think any kitchen-maid would accost a man like you did? Have you ever seen any girl of my class offer her body like that? I've only seen it among animals and prostitutes.

Miss Julie (*crushed*)   You're right. Hit me, trample on me, I've deserved nothing better. I'm worthless – but help me, help me out of this – if there is a way out.

Jean (*more gently*)   I don't want to disclaim my share in the honour of having seduced you, but do you imagine a man in my position would have dared to so much as glance at you if you hadn't invited him? I'm still dumbfounded –

Miss Julie   And proud.

Jean   Why not? Though I must confess I found the conquest a little too easy to be really exciting.

Miss Julie   Hurt me more.

Jean (*gets up*)   No. Forgive me for what I've said. I don't hit defenceless people, least of all women. I can't deny it gratifies me to have found that it was only a gilt veneer that dazzled our humble eyes, that the eagle's back was as scabbed as our own, that the whiteness of those cheeks was only powder, that those polished fingernails had black edges, that that handkerchief was dirty though it smelt of perfume – But on the other hand, it hurts me to have discovered that what I was aspiring towards was not something worthier and more solid. It hurts me to see you sunk so low, to find that deep down you are a kitchen slut. It hurts me, like seeing the autumn flowers whipped to tatters by the rain and trodden into the mud.

Miss Julie You speak as though you were already above me.

Jean I am. You see, I could make you into a countess, but you could never make me into a count.

Miss Julie But I am of noble blood, and you can never be that.

Jean That's true. But my children could be noblemen, if –

Miss Julie But you're a thief. That's something I am not.

Jean There are worse things than being a thief. Besides, when I work in a house I regard myself more or less as a member of the family, a child of the house, and people don't call it stealing when a child takes a berry from a bush heavy with fruit. (*His passion rises again.*) Miss Julie, you're a fine woman, much too good for someone like me. You've been the victim of a drunken folly, and you want to cover it up by pretending to yourself that you love me. You don't, unless perhaps physically – and then your love is no better than mine – but I can never be content with being just your animal, and I can never make you love me.

Miss Julie Are you sure of that?

Jean You mean it might happen? Yes, I could love you easily – you're beautiful, you're refined – (*He approaches her and takes her hand.*) Educated, lovable when you want to be, and once you have awoken a man's passion, it could never die. (*He puts his arm round her waist.*) You are like hot wine, strongly spiced, and a kiss from you – ! (*He tries to lead her out but she slowly tears herself free.*)

Miss Julie Let me go! You won't win me like that!

Jean   How, then? Not like that. Not by caresses and fine words. Not by thinking of your future, rescuing you from what you've done. How, then?

Miss Julie   How? How? I don't know. There is no way. I detest you as I detest rats, but I cannot run away from you.

Jean   Run away with me!

Miss Julie (*straightens herself*)   Run away? Yes, we must run away. But I'm so tired. Give me a glass of wine. I'm so tired. (**Jean** *pours her some. She looks at her watch.*) But we must talk first. We have a little time. (*She drains the glass and holds it out for more.*)

Jean   Don't drink so much, you'll get drunk.

Miss Julie   What does that matter?

Jean   What does it matter? It's stupid to get drunk. What were you going to say to me just now?

Miss Julie   We must run away! But first we must talk – that is, I must talk – so far you've been doing all the talking. You've told me about your life, now I must tell you about myself, so that we know all about each other before we go away together.

Jean   One moment. Forgive me, but – consider – you may later regret having revealed your private secrets to me.

Miss Julie   Aren't you my friend?

Jean   Yes – sometimes. But don't rely on me.

Miss Julie   You're only saying that. Anyway, everyone else knows. You see, my mother was a commoner, of quite humble birth. She was brought up with ideas about equality, freedom for women and all that. And she had a decided aversion to marriage. So when my father proposed to her, she replied that she would never become his wife, but that he could become her lover. My father told her that he had no desire to see the woman he loved enjoy less respect than himself. When she explained that the world's respect did not concern her, he agreed to her conditions. But now he was cut off from his social circle and confined to his domestic life, which could not satisfy him. And then? I came into the world, against my mother's wish as far as I can gather. She wanted to bring me up as a child of nature, and into the bargain I was to learn everything that a boy has to learn, so that I might stand as an example of how a woman can be as good as a man. I had to wear boy's clothes, and learn to look after horses – though I was never allowed to enter the cowshed. I had to groom and saddle them, and hunt – even learn to slaughter animals. That was horrible. Meanwhile, on the estate, all the men were set to perform the women's tasks, and the women the men's – so that it began to fail, and we became the laughing-stock of the district. In the end my father put his foot down, and everything was changed back to the way he wanted it. That was when they married. Then my mother fell ill – what illness, I don't know – but she often had convulsions, hid herself, in the attic and the garden, and sometimes stayed out all night. Then there was the great fire which you have heard about. The house, the stables and the cowshed were all burned down, under circumstances suggesting arson – for the accident happened the very day our quarterly insurance had expired, and the premium my father sent had been delayed through the inefficiency of the servant carrying it, so that it hadn't arrived in time. (*She fills her glass and drinks.*)

Jean   Don't drink so much.

Miss Julie   Oh, what does it matter? So we were left penniless, and had to sleep in the carriages. My father couldn't think where he would be able to find the money to rebuild the house, as he'd cut himself off from his old friends. Then mother advised him to ask for a loan from an old friend of hers, a brick merchant who lived in the neighbourhood. Father got the money, free of interest, which rather surprised him. So the house was rebuilt. (*She drinks again.*) Do you know who burned the house down?

Jean   Your mother!

Miss Julie   Do you know who the brick merchant was?

Jean   Your mother's lover!

Miss Julie   Do you know whose the money was?

Jean   Wait a moment. No, that I don't know.

Miss Julie   It was my mother's.

Jean   His lordship's too, then. Unless he'd made a marriage settlement.

Miss Julie   No, there wasn't any marriage settlement. My mother had had a little money of her own, which she didn't want my father to have control of. So she entrusted it to her – friend.

Jean   Who kept it!

Miss Julie   Exactly. He kept it. All this came to my father's knowledge – but he couldn't start an action, repay his wife's lover, or prove that the money was his wife's. It was my mother's revenge on him, for taking control of the house out of her hands. He was on the verge of shooting himself – the rumour was that he had done so, but had failed to kill himself. Well, he lived; and he made my mother pay for what she had done. Those five years were dreadful for me, I can tell you. I was sorry for my father, but I took my mother's side, because I didn't know the circumstances. I'd learned from her to distrust and hate men – she hated men. And I swore to her that I would never be a slave to any man.

Jean   But then you got engaged to that young lawyer?

Miss Julie   So that he should be my slave.

Jean   And he wasn't willing?

Miss Julie   He was willing enough, but he didn't get the chance. I tired of him.

Jean   I saw it. In the stable.

Miss Julie   Saw what?

Jean   How he broke off the engagement.

Miss Julie   That's a lie! It was I who broke it off! Has he been saying he did it, the little liar?

Jean   He wasn't a liar. You hate men, Miss Julie.

Miss Julie   Yes. Most of the time. But sometimes – when nature burns – ! Oh, God! Will the fire never die?

Jean   You hate me too?

Miss Julie   Immeasurably! I'd like to shoot you like an animal –

Jean   'The offender gets two years' penal servitude and the animal is shot.' That's the law for bestiality, isn't it? But you've nothing to shoot with. So what do you do?

Miss Julie

Jean   T

Miss Julie   eek – as long as one

Jean   than do that.

Miss Julie   , where the sun alw   ristmas, and the orang

Jean   Actua   ke of Como, and I never saw any oran   the grocers' shops. But it's a good spot for tourists, there   lot of villas to hire out to loving couples, and that's a pro   le industry – you know why? Because they lease them for six months, and then leave after three weeks.

Miss Julie (*naively*)   Why after three weeks?

Jean   They quarrel, of course! But they have to pay the full rent, and then you hire it out again. So it goes on, couple after couple. For love must go on, if not for very long.

Miss Julie   You don't want to die with me?

Jean   I don't want to die at all. Partly because I like life, and partly because I regard suicide as a crime against the Providence which gave us life.

Miss Julie   You believe in God – *you*?

Jean   Certainly I do. And I go to church every other Sunday. Quite frankly now, I'm tired of all this, and I'm going to bed.

Miss Julie   I see. And you think I'm going to rest content with that? Don't you know what a man owes to a woman he has shamed?

Jean (*takes out his purse and throws a silver coin on the table*)   Here. I always pay my debts.

Miss Julie (*pretends not to notice the insult*)   Do you know what the law says – ?

Jean   Unfortunately the law doesn't demand any penalty from a woman who seduces a man.

Miss Julie   Can you see any other solution than that we should go away, marry, and part?

Jean   And if I refuse to enter into this *mésalliance*?

Miss Julie   *Mésalliance?*

Jean   Yes – for me! I've got a better heritage than you. None of my ancestors committed arson.

Miss Julie   How do you know?

Jean   You couldn't prove it, because we don't have any family records – except with the police. But I've studied your pedigree in a book I found on the table in the drawing room. Do you know who the first of your ancestors to get a title was? He was a miller who let the king sleep with his wife one night during the Danish war. I haven't any noble ancestors like that – I haven't any noble ancestors at all. But I could become one myself.

Miss Julie   This is my reward for opening my heart to a servant, for giving my family's honour – !

Jean   Honour? Don't say I didn't tell you. One shouldn't drink, it loosens the tongue. And that's bad.

Miss Julie   Oh God, how I regret it, how I regret it! If you at least loved me – !

Jean   For the last time – what do you want? Shall I burst into

tears, shall I jump over your riding crop, shall I kiss you, trick
you down to Lake Como for three weeks, and then – what?
What shall I do? What do you want me to do? This is beginning
to get tiresome. It's always like this when one gets involved with
women. Miss Julie! I see you are unhappy, I know you are
suffering, but I do not understand you! We don't fool around like
you do – we don't hate – love is a game we play when we have a
little time free from work, but we aren't free all day and all night
like you! I think you must be ill. Yes, undoubtedly, you're ill.

Miss Julie   Speak kindly to me, Jean. Treat me like a human
being.

Jean   Act like one yourself, then. You spit at me, and won't let
me wipe it off – on you.

Miss Julie   Help me, help me! Just tell me what to do. Where
shall I go?

Jean   For God's sake! If I only knew!

Miss Julie   I've been mad, I know I've been mad, but isn't
there some way out?

Jean   Stay here, and keep calm. No one knows.

Miss Julie   Impossible. The servants know. And Christine.

Jean   They don't know for sure. They wouldn't really believe it
could happen.

Miss Julie (*hesitantly*)   But – it could happen again.

Jean   That is true.

Miss Julie   And – then?

Jean (*frightened*)   Then? My God, why didn't I think of that?
Yes, there's only one answer – you must go away. At once. I
can't come with you – then we'd be finished – you must go alone
– far away – anywhere.

Miss Julie   Alone? Where? I can't!

Jean   You must! And before his lordship returns. If you stay,
you know what'll happen. Once one has made a mistake one

wants to go on, because the damage has already been done. Then one gets more and more careless and – in the end one gets found out. So go! You can write to his lordship later and tell him everything – except that it was me! He'll never guess that. And I don't suppose he'll be over-keen to find out who it was.

Miss Julie   I'll go, if you'll come with me.

Jean   Are you mad, woman? Miss Julie run away with her servant! It'd be in the newspapers in a couple of days, and his lordship'd never live that down.

Miss Julie   I can't go. I can't stay. Help me! I'm so tired, so dreadfully tired. Order me! Make me do something! I can't think, I can't act –

Jean   Now you see what a contemptible creature you are! Why do you prink yourselves up and stick your noses in the air as though you were the lords of creation? Very well, I shall order you. Go up to your room, get dressed, get some money for the journey and come back here.

Miss Julie (*half-whispers*)   Come with me.

Jean   To your room? Now you're being crazy again. (*He hesitates for a moment.*) No! Go, at once! (*He takes her hand and leads her out.*)

Miss Julie (*as she goes*)   Speak kindly to me, Jean!

Jean   An order always sounds unkind. Now you know how it feels!

Jean, *left alone, heaves a sigh of relief, sits at the table, takes out a notebook and pencil, and makes some calculations muttering occasionally to himself.*

Dumb mime, until **Christine** *enters, dressed for church, with a man's dickey and white tie in her hand.*

Christine   Blessed Jesus, what a mess! What on earth have you been up to?

Jean   Oh, it was Miss Julie – she brought the servants in. You must have been fast asleep – didn't you hear anything?

Christine   I slept like a log.

Jean   Dressed for church already?

Christine   Yes. You promised to come with me to Communion this morning.

Jean   So I did. And I see you've brought the uniform. OK, then.

He sits. **Christine** *dresses him in his dickey and white tie. Pause.*

Jean (*sleepily*)   What's the lesson today?

Christine   Execution of John the Baptist, I expect.

Jean   Oh God, that's a long one. Hi, you're strangling me! Oh, I'm so tired, so tired.

Christine   Well, what have you been doing, up all night? You're quite green in the face.

Jean   Sitting here, talking with Miss Julie.

Christine   She doesn't know what's right and proper, that one.

Pause.

Jean   I say, Christine.

Christine   Mm?

Jean   It's strange, you know, when you think of it. Her.

Christine   What's strange?

Jean   Everything.

Pause.

Christine (*sees the glasses, half empty, on the table*)   Have you been drinking together, too?

Jean   Yes.

Christine   For shame! Look me in the eyes!

Jean   Yes?

Christine   Is it possible? Is it *possible?*

Jean (*after a moment*)   Yes.

Christine   Ugh! *That* I'd never have believed! No! Shame on you, shame!

Jean   You aren't jealous of her, are you?

Christine   No, not of her! If it had been Clara or Sophie – then I'd have torn your eyes out. But her – no – I don't know why. Ah, but it's disgusting!

Jean   Are you angry with her, then?

Christine   No, with you! It's a wicked thing to have done, wicked! Poor lass! No, I don't care who hears it, I don't want to stay any longer in a house where people can't respect their employers.

Jean   Why should one respect them?

Christine   Yes, you're so clever, you tell me! But you don't want to work for people who lower themselves, do you? Eh? You lower yourself by it, that's my opinion.

Jean   Yes, but it's a comfort for us to know they aren't any better than us.

Christine   Not to my mind. If they're no better than we are there's no point our trying to improve ourselves. And think of his lordship! Think of him and all the misery he's had in his time! No, I don't want to stay in this house any longer. Blessed Jesus! And with someone like you! If it'd been that young lawyer fellow – if it'd been a gentleman –

Jean   What's wrong with me?

Christine   Oh, you're all right in your way, but there's a difference between people and people. No, I'll never be able to forget this. Miss Julie, who was always so proud, so cool with men – I never thought she'd go and give herself to someone – and to someone like you! She, who all but had poor Diana shot for running after the gatekeeper's pug! Yes, I'm not afraid to say it! I won't stay here any longer. On the 24th of October I go!

Jean   And then?

Christine   Yes, since you've raised the subject, it's time you started looking round for something, seeing as we're going to get married.

Jean   What kind of thing? I can't have a job like this once I'm married.

Christine   No, of course not. Still, you might get something as a porter, or maybe a caretaker in some government office. A bird in the hand's worth two in the bush; and there'll be a pension for your wife and children.

Jean (*grimaces*)   Yes, that's all very fine, but I don't intend to die to oblige my wife and children just yet, thank you very much. I've higher ambitions than that.

Christine   Ambitions? What about your responsibilities? Think of them.

Jean   Oh, shut up about responsibilities, I know my duty. (*He listens towards the door.*) But we've plenty of time to think about that. Go inside now and get yourself ready, and we'll go to church.

Christine   Who's that walking about upstairs?

Jean   I don't know. Probably Clara.

Christine (*going*)   It surely can't be his lordship. He couldn't have come back without our hearing him.

Jean (*frightened*)   His lordship? No, it can't be, he'd have rung.

Christine (*goes*)   Well, God help us. I've never been mixed up in the likes of this before.

The sun has now risen and is shining on the tops of the trees in the park. Its beams move gradually until they fall at an angle through the windows. **Jean** *goes to the door and makes a sign.*

Miss Julie (*enters in travelling clothes with a small birdcage, covered with a cloth, which she places on a chair*)   I'm ready now.

Jean   Ssh! Christine is awake!

Miss Julie (*very nervous throughout this dialogue*)   Does she suspect anything?

Jean   She knows nothing. But, my God – what a sight you look!

Miss Julie   What's wrong – ?

Jean   You're as white as a corpse, and – forgive me, but your face is dirty.

Miss Julie   Let me wash, then. Here. (*She goes to the washbasin and washes her face and hands*.) Give me a towel. Oh – the sun's rising!

Jean   And then the Devil loses his power.

Miss Julie   Yes, the Devil's been at work tonight. But Jean, listen. Come with me! I've got some money now.

Jean (*doubtfully*)   Enough?

Miss Julie   Enough to start with! Come with me! I can't go alone, not today. Think – Midsummer Day, on a stuffy train, squashed among crowds of people staring at me – having to stand still on stations, when one longs to be flying away! No, I can't, I can't! And then – memories – memories of midsummers in childhood, the church garlanded with birch-leaves and lilac, dinner at the long table, the family, friends – the afternoons in the park, dancing, music, flowers, games! Oh, one runs, one runs away, but memories follow in the baggage-wagon – and remorse – and guilt!

Jean   I'll come with you – but it must be now, at once, before it's too late. Now, this minute!

Miss Julie   Get dressed, then. (*She picks up the birdcage*.)

Jean   No luggage, though. That'd give us away.

Miss Julie   No, nothing. Only what we can have in the compartment with us.

Jean (*has taken his hat*)   What have you got there? What is it?

Miss Julie   It's only my greenfinch. I don't want to leave her.

Jean   For heaven's sake! We can't take a birdcage with us now.
You're crazy. Put that cage down.

Miss Julie   My one memory of home – the only living thing
that loves me, since Diana was unfaithful to me. Don't be cruel!
Let me take her with me!

Jean   Put that cage down, I tell you. And don't talk so loud,
Christine will hear us.

Miss Julie   No I won't leave her for strangers to have. I'd
rather you killed her.

Jean   Bring the little beast here then, and I will.

Miss Julie   All right – but don't hurt her. Don't – no, I can't!

Jean   Bring it here. I can.

Miss Julie (*takes the bird out of its cage and kisses it*)   Ah, poor little
Serina, are you going to die now and leave your mistress?

Jean   Please don't make a scene. Your life and your happiness
are at stake. Here, quickly! (*He snatches the bird from her, takes it to the
chopping block and picks up the kitchen axe.* **Miss Julie** *turns away.*)
You ought to have learned how to wring chickens' necks instead
of how to fire a pistol. (*He brings down the axe.*) Then you wouldn't
have been frightened of a drop of blood.

Miss Julie (*screams*)   Kill me too! Kill me! You, who can
slaughter an innocent creature without a tremor! Oh, I hate and
detest you! There is blood between us now! I curse the moment I
set eyes on you, I curse the moment I was conceived in my
mother's womb!

Jean   What's the good of cursing? Come!

Miss Julie (*goes towards the chopping block, as though drawn against her
will*)   No, I don't want to go yet. I can't – I must see – ssh!
There's a carriage outside! (*She listens, but keeps her eyes fixed all the
while on the chopping block and the axe.*) Do you think I can't bear the
sight of blood? You think I'm so weak – oh, I should like to see
your blood, your brains, on a chopping block – I'd like to see all
your sex swimming in a lake of blood – I think I could drink from

your skull, I'd like to bathe my feet in your guts, I could eat your heart, roasted! You think I'm weak – you think I loved you, because my womb wanted your seed, you think I want to carry your embryo under my heart and feed it with my blood, bear your child and take your name! By the way, what is your surname! I've never heard it – you probably haven't any. I'd have to be 'Mrs Kitchen-boy', or 'Mrs Lavatory man' – you dog, who wear my collar, you lackey who carry my crest on your buttons – am I to share with my own cook, compete with a scullery slut? Oh, oh, oh! You think I'm a coward and want to run away? No, now I shall stay. Let the storm break! My father will come home – find his desk broken open – his money gone! He'll ring – this bell – twice, for his lackey – then he'll send for the police – and I shall tell everything. Everything. Oh, it'll be good to end it all – if only it could be the end. And then he'll have a stroke and die. Then we shall all be finished, and there'll be peace – peace – eternal rest! And the coat of arms will be broken over the coffin – the title extinct – and the lackey's line will be carried on in an orphanage, win laurels in the gutter, and end in a prison!

Jean   That's the blue blood talking! Bravo, Miss Julie! Just give the miller a rest, now – !

Christine *enters, dressed for church, with a prayer-book in her hand.*
Miss Julie *runs towards her and falls into her arms, as though seeking shelter.*

Miss Julie   Help me, Christine! Help me against this man!

Christine (*motionless, cold*)   What kind of a spectacle's this on a Sunday morning? (*She looks at the chopping block.*) And what a pigsty you've made here. What does all this mean? I never heard such shouting and bawling.

Miss Julie   Christine! Christine, listen to me and I'll explain everything.

Jean (*somewhat timid and embarrassed*)   While you ladies discuss the matter, I'll go inside and shave. (*He slips out right.*)

Miss Julie   You must try to understand! You must listen to me!

Christine   No, this kind of thing I don't understand. Where are you going in those clothes? And what's he doing with his hat on – eh? – eh?

Miss Julie   Listen to me, Christine. Listen, and I'll explain everything –

Christine   I don't want to know anything –

Miss Julie   You must listen to me –

Christine   About what? What you've done with Jean? That doesn't bother me – that's between you and him. But if you're thinking of trying to fool him into running away, we'll soon put a stop to that.

Miss Julie (*very nervous*)   Now try to be calm, Christine, and listen to me. I can't stay here, and Jean can't stay here – so we have to go –

Christine   Hm, hm!

Miss Julie (*becoming brighter*)   Listen, I've just had an idea – why don't we all three go away – abroad – to Switzerland – and start a hotel together – I've money, you see – and Jean and I could run it – and you, I thought you might take charge of the kitchen – isn't that a good idea? Say yes, now! And come with us, and then everything'll be settled! Say yes, now!

Christine (*coldly, thoughtfully*)   Hm, hm!

Miss Julie (*speaks very rapidly*)   You've never been abroad, Christine – you must get away from here and see the world. You've no idea what fun it is to travel by train – new people all the time – new countries – we'll go through Hamburg and look at the zoo – you'll like that – and then we'll go to the theatre and listen to the opera – and when we get to Munich there'll be all the museums, Christine, and Rubens and Raphael, those great painters, you know – you've heard of Munich – where King Ludwig lived, you know, the King who went mad. And we'll see his palaces – they've still got palaces there, just like in the fairy tales – and from there it isn't far to Switzerland – and the Alps, Christine – fancy, the Alps, with snow on them in the middle of

summer – and oranges grow there, and laurel trees that are
green all the year round –

Jean *can be seen in the wings right, whetting his razor on a strop which he holds between his teeth and his left hand. He listens contentedly to what is being said, every now and then nodding his approval.*

Miss Julie (*more rapidly still*)   And we'll start a hotel there – I'll sit at the desk while Jean stands in the doorway and receives the guests – I'll go out and do the shopping – and write the letters – oh Christine, what a life it'll be! The trains will whistle, and then the buses'll arrive, and bells will ring on all the floors and in the restaurant – and I'll write out the bills – and salt them, too – you can't imagine how timid tourists are when they have to pay the bill! And you – you'll be in charge of the kitchen – you won't have to do any cooking yourself, of course – and you'll wear fine clothes, for the guests to see you in – and you, with your looks, I'm not flattering you, Christine, you'll get yourself a husband one fine day, a rich Englishman, you'll see – English people are so easy to – (*slowing down*) – catch – and we'll become rich – and build ourselves a villa on Lake Como – it rains there sometimes, of course, but – (*slows right down*) – the sun must shine there too, sometimes – though it looks dark – and – so – if it doesn't we can come home again – back to – (*Pause.*) Back here – or somewhere –

Christine   Now listen. Do you believe all this?

Miss Julie (*crushed*)   Do I believe it?

Christine   Yes.

Miss Julie (*wearily*)   I don't know. I don't believe in anything any longer. (*She falls on to the bench and puts her head on the table between her hands.*) Nothing. Nothing at all.

Christine (*turns right to where* **Jean** *is standing*)   So! You were thinking of running away!

Jean (*crestfallen, puts his razor down on the table*)   Running away? Oh now, that's exaggerating. You heard Miss Julie's plan and although she's tired now after being up all night I think it's a very practical proposition.

Christine Listen to him! Did you expect me to act as cook to that – ?

Jean (*sharply*) Kindly express yourself respectfully when you refer to your mistress. Understand?

Christine Mistress!

Jean Yes.

Christine Listen to him, listen to him!

Jean Yes, listen to me, and talk a little less. Miss Julie is your mistress, and what you despise in her you should despise in yourself too.

Christine I've always had sufficient respect for myself –

Jean To be able to turn up your nose at others.

Christine To stop me from demeaning myself. You tell me when you've seen his lordship's cook mucking around with the groom or the pigman! Just you tell me!

Jean Yes, you managed to get hold of a gentleman for yourself. You were lucky.

Christine Yes, a gentleman who sells his lordship's oats, which he steals from the stables –

Jean You should talk! You take a percentage on all the groceries, and a rake-off from the butcher –

Christine What!

Jean And you say you can't respect your employers! You, you, you!

Christine Are you coming with me to church now? You need a good sermon after what you've done.

Jean No, I'm not going to church today. You can go by yourself, and confess what you've been up to.

Christine Yes, I will, and I'll come home with my sins forgiven, and yours too. The blessed Saviour suffered and died on the cross for all our sins, and if we turn to Him with a loyal and humble heart He'll take all our sins upon Him.

Jean   Including the groceries?

Miss Julie   Do you believe that, Christine?

Christine   With all my heart, as surely as I stand here. I learned it as a child, Miss Julie, and I've believed it ever since. And where the sin is exceeding great, there His mercy shall overflow.

Miss Julie   Oh, if only I had your faith! Oh, if – !

Christine   Ah, but you can't have that except by God's special grace, and that isn't granted to everyone –

Miss Julie   Who has it, then?

Christine   That's God's great secret, Miss Julie. And the Lord's no respecter of persons. There shall the last be first –

Miss Julie   Then He has respect for the last?

Christine (*continues*)   And it is easier for a camel to pass through the eye of a needle than for a rich man to enter the Kingdom of Heaven. That's how it is, Miss Julie. Well, I'll be going – and as I pass the stable I'll tell the groom not to let any of the horses be taken out before his lordship comes home, just in case. Goodbye. (*She goes.*)

Jean   Damned bitch! And all for a greenfinch!

Miss Julie (*dully*)   Never mind the greenfinch. Can you see any way out of this, any end to it?

Jean (*thinks*)   No.

Miss Julie   What would you do in my place?

Jean   In your place? Wait, now. If I was a lady – of noble birth – who'd fallen – ? I don't know. Yes. I do know.

Miss Julie (*picks up the razor and makes a gesture*)   This?

Jean   Yes. But *I* wouldn't do it, mind. There's a difference between us.

Miss Julie   Because you're a man and I am a woman? What difference does that make?

Jean   The difference – between a man and a woman.

Miss Julie (*holding the razor*)   I want to do it – but I can't. My father couldn't do it, either, the time he should have.

Jean   No, he was right. He had to be revenged first.

Miss Julie   And now my mother will be revenged again, through me.

Jean   Have you never loved your father, Miss Julie?

Miss Julie   Yes – enormously – but I've hated him too. I must have done so without realising it. But it was he who brought me up to despise my own sex, made me half woman and half man. Who is to blame for what has happened – my father, my mother, myself? Myself? I have no self. I haven't a thought I didn't get from my father, not an emotion I didn't get from my mother – and this last idea – that all people are equal – I got that from him, my fiancé whom I called a wretched little fool because of it. How can the blame be mine, then? Put it all on to Jesus, as Christine did – no, I'm too proud to do that, and too clever – thanks to my learned father. And that about a rich person not being able to get into heaven, that's a lie, and Christine has money in the savings bank so she won't get there either. Whose fault is it all? What does it matter to us whose fault it is? I shall have to bear the blame, carry the consequences –

Jean   Yes, but –

There are two sharp rings on the bell. **Miss Julie** *jumps up.* **Jean** *changes his coat.*

Jean   His lordship's home! Good God, do you suppose Christine – ? (*Goes to the speaking-tube, knocks on it, and listens.*)

Miss Julie   Has he been to his desk?

Jean   It's Jean, milord. (*He listens. The audience cannot hear what is said to him.*) Yes, milord. (*He listens.*) Yes, milord. Immediately. (*He* *listens.*) At once, milord. (*Listens.*) Very good, my lord. In half an hour.

Miss Julie (*desperately frightened*)   What does he say? For God's sake, what does he say?

Jean   He wants his boots and his coffee in half an hour.

Miss Julie   In half an hour, then – ! Oh, I'm so tired! I can't feel anything, I can't repent, can't run away, can't stay, can't live – can't die. Help me! Order me, and I'll obey you like a dog. Do me this last service, save my honour, save his name! You know what I ought to will myself to do, but I can't. Will me to, Jean, order me!

Jean   I don't know – now I can't either – I don't understand – it's just as though this coat made me – I *can't* order you – and now, since his lordship spoke to me – I can't explain it properly, but – oh, it's this damned lackey that sits on my back – I think if his lordship came down now and ordered me to cut my throat, I'd do it on the spot.

Miss Julie   Then pretend that you are he, and I am you. You acted so well just now, when you went down on your knees – then you were an aristocrat – or – haven't you ever been to the theatre and seen a hypnotist? (**Jean** *nods.*) He says to his subject: 'Take the broom!' and he takes it. He says: 'Sweep!' and he sweeps –

Jean   But the subject has to be asleep.

Miss Julie (*in an ecstasy*)   I am already asleep – the whole room is like smoke around me – and you look like an iron stove – which resembles a man dressed in black, with a tall hat – and your eyes shine like coals, when the fire is dying – and your face is a white smear, like ash – (*The sun's rays have now reached the floor and are shining on* **Jean**.) It's so warm and good – ! (*She rubs her hands as though warming them before a fire.*) And so bright – and so peaceful – !

Jean (*takes the razor and places it in her hand*)   Here's the broom. Go now – while it's light – out to the barn – and – (*He whispers in her ear.*)

Miss Julie (*awake*)   Thank you. Now I am going to rest. But just tell me this – those who are first – they too can receive grace? Say it to me – even if you don't believe it.

Jean   Those who are first? No, I can't! But, wait – Miss Julie – now I see it! You are no longer among the first. You are – among the last!

Miss Julie   That's true. I am among the last of all. I am the last. Oh! But now I can't go! Tell me once more – say I must go!

Jean   No, now I can't either. I can't!

Miss Julie   And the first shall be last.

Jean   Don't think, don't think! You take all my strength from me, you make me a coward. What? I thought the bell moved! No. Shall we stuff paper in it? To be so afraid of a bell! Yes, but it isn't only a bell – there's someone sitting behind it – a hand sets it in motion – and something else sets the hand in motion – you've only got to close your ears, close your ears! Yes, but now he's ringing louder! He'll ring till someone answers – and then it'll be too late. The police will come – and then – !

Two loud rings on the bell.

Jean (*cringes, then straightens himself up*)   It's horrible. But it's the only possible ending. Go!

Miss Julie *walks firmly out through the door.*

Notes

xciii   *on the bench*: becomes a judge or magistrate.
  xcv   *the Goncourt brothers*: Edmond Louis Antoine Huot and Jules
        Alfred Huot de Goncourt were famous for their jointly
        authored Naturalist novels, including *Germinie Lacerteux*
        (1864) and *Mme Gervaisais* (1869). They were also
        successful art critics and cultural historians who published
        their *Journal des Goncourt* about artistic life in Paris from
        1851 to 1896. Edmond left money at his death to found
        the Goncourt Academy which makes an annual award for
        fiction, the Goncourt Prize.
 xcvi   *the Italian theatre has, in certain instances, returned to improvisation*:
        Strindberg is probably thinking of the work of the
        eighteenth-century playwright Carlo Gozzi who made a
        determined attempt to restore the tradition of
        improvisation based on the *commedia dell'arte* traditions of
        stock characters.
xcvii   Strindberg's innovative ideas on stage setting and acting
        are inspired by the example of André Antoine and his
        Théâtre Libre founded in 1887 in Paris.

        The Play
    3   *scalloped paper*: the shelves are lined with paper that has
        decorative scalloped edges. In some Scandinavian
        kitchens, lace edgings are used instead of scalloped paper.
    4   *Ceci est mon grand délice*: 'This is my favourite dish.' Jean has
        learnt French during a stay in Switzerland, when he was
        wine waiter at the biggest hotel in Lucerne.
    6   *schottische*: a popular energetic dance involving a
        combination of two movements, a polka and a circular
        hop. The hopping movement involves a step and a hop on
        each foot alternately while turning clockwise in place.
    9   *Très gentil*: 'very elegant.'
        Vous voulez plaisanter: 'Is that meant as a joke?'
   13   *We must sleep with nine midsummer flowers under our pillows
        tonight*: folklore dictated that unmarried maidens who slept
        with nine midsummer flowers under their pillow on
        Midsummer Eve would dream of the man they were to
        marry.

13 *Attention. Je ne suis qu'un homme!*: 'Don't forget that I'm a man.'

14 *Joseph*: the taunting reference is to the story of Joseph and Potiphar's wife in Genesis 39: 7–15: 'Now Joseph was handsome and good-looking, and a time came when his master's wife took notice of him and said, "Come and lie with me." But he refused and said to her, "Think of my master. He does not know as much as I do about his own house, and he has entrusted me with all he has. He has given me authority in this house second only to his own, and has withheld nothing from me except you, because you are his wife. How can I do anything so wicked, and sin against God?" She kept asking Joseph day after day, but he refused to lie with her and be in her company. One day he came into the house as usual to do his work, when none of the men of the household were there indoors. She caught him by his cloak, saying, "Come and lie with me", but he left the cloak in her hands and ran out of the house. When she saw that he had left his cloak in her hands and had run out of the house, she called out to the men of the household, "Look at this! My husband has brought in a Hebrew to make a mockery of us. He came in here to lie with me, but I gave a loud scream. When he heard me scream and call out, he left his cloak in my hand and ran off." The comparison is meant to provoke Jean, which it does. But Jean soon proves that he does not share either Joseph's sense of duty or his morality.

15 *Garden of Paradise . . . Tree of Life*: the reference is to the biblical Garden of Eden and the Tree of the Knowledge of Good and Evil. 'The Lord God took the man and put him in the Garden of Eden to till it and care for it. He told the man, "You may eat from every tree in the garden, but not from the Tree of the Knowledge of Good and Evil; for on the day that you eat from it, you will certainly die"' (Genesis 2: 15–18).

16 *enfin*: 'well . . .' Jean's words suggest a sexual, masturbatory motive for his second visit to the splendid garden toilet.

16 *a thief can enter heaven*: Jean is alluding to the crucifixion of Jesus when one of the thieves crucified alongside Jesus

said, 'Remember me when you come into your kingdom.'
Jesus replied, 'I promise you today you will be with me in
paradise' (Luke 23: 42–3).

17 *oat-bin*: the oat-bin offers a relatively airtight space, so that
the supposed poisonous effect of the elderflowers can take
effect. In fact elderflowers are not poisonous but are
sometimes described as having a narcotic perfume that is
suggestive of death.

24 *Merde*: 'Piss off!' (literally, 'Shit!').

30 The reference to the criminal offence of bestiality confirms
that Jean has behaved towards her like an animal. If he
really were an animal, as she suggests, he would be shot
and she would face a prison sentence.

34 *Execution of John the Baptist*: the suggested reading on the
execution of John the Baptist is an ironic reference to what
is to happen in the action of the play: namely, Miss Julie's
greenfinch is to be beheaded and she herself is to cut her
own throat. John had rebuked Herod for marrying
Herodias, the wife of his half-brother. Herodias never
forgot this and was determined to be revenged on John.
Her opportunity came when her daughter Salome pleased
Herod by dancing for him and his guests. Herod promised
her that she could have anything she wished. Herodias
instructed Salome to ask for John's head on a dish. Herod
granted her request. 'Because of his oath, and because of
them that were with him at table, he would not displease
her: but sending an executioner, he commanded that his
head should be brought in a dish: and gave it to the
damsel, and the damsel gave it to her mother' (Mark 6:
21–8). The festival that is actually celebrated on
Midsummer Day in Sweden is the birth of John the
Baptist. The reading for that festival would be from Luke
1: 57–66 which describes Elizabeth giving birth and
deciding to call her son John.

35 *Diana*: ironically, Miss Julie's bitch is named after the
chaste Roman goddess of hunting.

40 *King Ludwig*: the famously mad King of Bavaria had only
just finished building his fairy-tale castle of
Neuschwanstein in 1886. The Pinakothek in Munich has a

fine collection of European art, which Miss Julie has
presumably visited at some point with her father.
43 Christine's biblical references may be found in Matthew
20: 16: 'So the last will be first, and the first will be last';
and Matthew 19: 24: 'It is easier for a camel to go through
the eye of a needle than for a rich man to enter the
kingdom of God.'

Questions for Further Study

1. What kind of relationship does Jean have with Christine? What values do they have in common and in what ways do their views diverge?

2. How far do you think that Miss Julie is responsible for her own downfall?

3. In his desire to seduce Miss Julie, are Jean's motives primarily sexual or social?

4. *Miss Julie* is set in the kitchen of a Swedish manor house on Midsummer Eve. Discuss the importance of this setting for the action.

5. How far do you agree that the action of *Miss Julie* revolves primarily around class antagonism?

6. In what ways does the structure of *Miss Julie* mirror the rhythm of sexual arousal followed by the guilt-ridden aftermath of sexual intercourse?

7. If you were directing a production of *Miss Julie*, what advice would you give to those playing the roles of Jean and Miss Julie to help them understand the shifts of mood and status experienced by these characters and then to find an appropriate style of acting to convey these shifts?

8. Discuss whether *Miss Julie* can be seen as a genuinely Naturalistic tragedy.

9. In *Miss Julie*, there are striking visual images in the stage directions and in the dialogue. What light do they throw on the action?

10. Comment on the importance of non-verbal elements in the action of *Miss Julie*, notably in the scenes of mime and ballet and also in some of the gestures and blocking suggested in the stage directions.

11. How far can the behaviour of the characters in *Miss Julie* be seen as the product of environmental determinism?

12. In *Miss Julie*, in what ways do images of nature and comparisons between humans and animals serve to underline the notion that human behaviour is motivated by animal urges and instincts?

13. To what extent does the action of *Miss Julie* explore in an Expressionist manner the subjective dreams and fantasies of the two main protagonists?

14. The ending of *Miss Julie* seems to involve a complete shift of mood and style by comparison with earlier scenes. In what ways does Strindberg prepare an audience for this transition at earlier stages in the action?

15. Strindberg suggests in his Preface that *Miss Julie* could be read as a misogynistic attack on the man-hating half-woman. Do you agree?

16. Explore the significance of the sexually fetishised objects referred to or shown in the action of *Miss Julie*. What do these fetishised objects suggest about the subtextual meaning of the play?

17. How far do you agree that in *Miss Julie* Strindberg shows all human social and sexual activity to be motivated by games of power and status?

18. In *Miss Julie* Strindberg shows nothing beyond 'the lust of the flesh and the incurable loneliness of the soul'. Discuss.

19. Strindberg's contemporaries rejected and shunned *Miss Julie*. In what ways does the action of the play challenge the values of late nineteenth-century bourgeois society?

20. In what ways does the action of *Miss Julie* embody the Nietzschean concept of an aesthetic transcendence of absurdity?

21. Compare and contrast *Miss Julie* with *Hedda Gabler*, commenting on the relative importance attached to free will and determinism in each play.

DAVID THOMAS was Professor and Chairman of Theatre Studies at the University of Warwick until his retirement in 2004. He is now a Professor Emeritus at Warwick. He has directed productions of plays by Ibsen, Strindberg, Dryden and Etherege and operas by Strauss, Donizetti, Mozart and Gluck. He has contributed to television programmes on Handel opera (*South Bank Show*) and the Drury Lane playhouse (Channel 4: *Lost Buildings of Britain*). His main publications include: *Henrik Ibsen* (Macmillan, 1983); *Theatre in Europe: A Documentary History. Restoration and Georgian England 1660–1788* (Cambridge University Press, 1989); and *William Congreve* (Macmillan, 1992). More recent publications include a video, *The Restoration Stage: from Tennis Court to Playhouse* (University of Warwick and Films for the Humanities, 1996), and two anthologies of plays, *Six Restoration and French Neoclassic Plays* and *Four Georgian and Pre-Revolutionary Plays* (Macmillan, 1998). He wrote the commentary and notes for the Methuen student edition of *Hedda Gabler* published in 2002.

JO TAYLOR graduated from the University of Warwick with a first-class degree in English and Theatre Studies in 2005. While at Warwick, she wrote a dissertation on Strindberg which David Thomas supervised. Her work on this volume involves a collaborative extension of their previously shared enthusiasm for Strindberg's work. During her time at Warwick she was involved in arts management at Warwick Arts Centre, Edinburgh Fringe Festival and the founding of the Warwick Student Arts Festival. Since graduating she has managed the marketing for Black Swan Arts in Somerset. Her next project is a travel journal of the arts in Sri Lanka and India.

The two authors contributed to the Commentary as follows: Jo took primary responsibility for 'The biographical context' and 'Strindberg's Naturalist trilogy'. David took primary responsibility for the Chronology, Plot, 'The Preface', 'The social context', 'The stage setting, stage directions and use of stage space', and '*Miss Julie* on stage'. Both authors shared the task of writing the commentary on 'The relationships'. David exercised editorial control over the volume as a whole.

Methuen Drama Student Editions

Jean Anouilh *Antigone* • John Arden *Serjeant Musgrave's Dance*
Alan Ayckbourn *Confusions* • Aphra Behn *The Rover* • Edward Bond
Lear • *Saved* • Bertolt Brecht *The Caucasian Chalk Circle* • *Fear and
Misery in the Third Reich* • *The Good Person of Szechwan* • *Life of Galileo* •
Mother Courage and her Children • *The Resistible Rise of Arturo Ui* • *The
Threepenny Opera* • Anton Chekhov *The Cherry Orchard* • *The Seagull* •
Three Sisters • *Uncle Vanya* • Caryl Churchill *Serious Money* • *Top Girls*
• Shelagh Delaney *A Taste of Honey* • Euripides *Elektra* • *Medea*•
Dario Fo *Accidental Death of an Anarchist* • Michael Frayn *Copenhagen*
• John Galsworthy *Strife* • Nikolai Gogol *The Government Inspector* •
Robert Holman *Across Oka* • Henrik Ibsen *A Doll's House* • *Ghosts*•
Hedda Gabler • Charlotte Keatley *My Mother Said I Never Should* •
Bernard Kops *Dreams of Anne Frank* • Federico García Lorca *Blood
Wedding* • *Doña Rosita the Spinster* (bilingual edition) •*The House of
Bernarda Alba* • (bilingual edition) • *Yerma* (bilingual edition) • David
Mamet *Glengarry Glen Ross* • *Oleanna* • Patrick Marber *Closer* • John
Marston *Malcontent* • Martin McDonagh *The Lieutenant of Inishmore* •
Joe Orton *Loot* • Luigi Pirandello *Six Characters in Search of an Author*
• Mark Ravenhill *Shopping and F***ing* • Willy Russell *Blood Brothers*
• *Educating Rita* • Sophocles *Antigone* • *Oedipus the King* • Wole
Soyinka *Death and the King's Horseman* • Shelagh Stephenson *The
Memory of Water* • August Strindberg *Miss Julie* • J. M. Synge *The
Playboy of the Western World* • Theatre Workshop *Oh What a Lovely
War* Timberlake Wertenbaker *Our Country's Good* • Arnold Wesker
The Merchant • Oscar Wilde *The Importance of Being Earnest* •
Tennessee Williams *A Streetcar Named Desire* • *The Glass Menagerie*

Methuen Drama Contemporary Dramatists

include

John Arden (two volumes)
Arden & D'Arcy
Peter Barnes (three volumes)
Sebastian Barry
Dermot Bolger
Edward Bond (eight volumes)
Howard Brenton
  (two volumes)
Richard Cameron
Jim Cartwright
Caryl Churchill (two volumes)
Sarah Daniels (two volumes)
Nick Darke
David Edgar (three volumes)
David Eldridge
Ben Elton
Dario Fo (two volumes)
Michael Frayn (three volumes)
David Greig
John Godber (four volumes)
Paul Godfrey
John Guare
Lee Hall (two volumes)
Peter Handke
Jonathan Harvey
  (two volumes)
Declan Hughes
Terry Johnson (three volumes)
Sarah Kane
Barrie Keeffe
Bernard-Marie Koltès
  (two volumes)
Franz Xaver Kroetz
David Lan
Bryony Lavery
Deborah Levy
Doug Lucie

David Mamet (four volumes)
Martin McDonagh
Duncan McLean
Anthony Minghella
  (two volumes)
Tom Murphy (six volumes)
Phyllis Nagy
Anthony Neilsen (two volumes)
Philip Osment
Gary Owen
Louise Page
Stewart Parker (two volumes)
Joe Penhall (two volumes)
Stephen Poliakoff
  (three volumes)
David Rabe (two volumes)
Mark Ravenhill (two volumes)
Christina Reid
Philip Ridley
Willy Russell
Eric-Emmanuel Schmitt
Ntozake Shange
Sam Shepard (two volumes)
Wole Soyinka (two volumes)
Simon Stephens (two volumes)
Shelagh Stephenson
David Storey (three volumes)
Sue Townsend
Judy Upton
Michel Vinaver
  (two volumes)
Arnold Wesker (two volumes)
Michael Wilcox
Roy Williams (three volumes)
Snoo Wilson (two volumes)
David Wood (two volumes)
Victoria Wood

For a complete catalogue of Methuen Drama titles
write to:

Methuen Drama
36 Soho Square
London
W1D 3QY

or you can visit our website at:

www.methuendrama.com